Praise for The Latin Table

"*The Latin Table* is more than cookbook; it is a compilation of beautiful photographs from the past to the present, easy-to-follow recipes that our family have all delighted in at our home celebrations, and beautiful stories revealing the human spirit. A nice combination of love in creation."

—Deepak and Rita Chopra

"This book should be called *The Latin 'Friends & Family Table* because it's everything you'd want to make for people you love. From her must-have Black Beans to the Shrimp Boil Latina Style and the Ropa Vieja, you'll get a real sense of the dishes that have influenced Isabel's life—dishes you'll want to make and share forever."

—Sam the Cooking Guy

"Isabel, can you adopt me, please? Isabel's boundless, infectious enthusiasm pairs with dead-simple recipes that are long on flamboyant flavor and color. This quintessential gateway book lets us get up close and personal with a delicious cuisine many of us already adore from afar."

—Brigit Binns, author of *Williams-Sonoma: Cooking in Season*,
Sunset's Eating Up the West Coast, and *The New Wine Country Cuisine*

"A seat at Isabel Cruz's *Latin Table* is an invitation to a world of flavor, fun, and nostalgia! Her recipes are healthy, vibrant, and filled with color. Isabel brings to life the sights, smells, and tastes of the cuisine from Latin America woven with their cultural roots and heartfelt stories. *The Latin Table* celebrates food, family, and life."

—Chef Bernard Guillas, executive chef/Maitre Cuisinier De France,
Académie De France, and author of *Flying Pans and Two Chefs, One Catch*

the Latin Table

EASY,
FLAVORFUL RECIPES FROM MEXICO,
PUERTO RICO, AND BEYOND

ISABEL CRUZ

PHOTOGRAPHS BY JAIME FRITSCH

Skyhorse Publishing

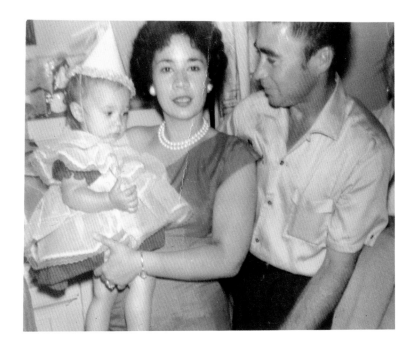

To the sweetest, best person I will ever know. How did I get so lucky that you are my momma!

Guava Rum Punch for Two, page 121

contents

Introduction

I am obsessed with Latin America: the warmth of the people, the architecture, the music, and especially the **food**! Latin cuisine is easy to make, tastes amazing, and is healthy—yes, healthy! I haven't always appreciated it, though.

Growing up in a Puerto Rican family, I remember my mother, my two brothers, and I ganging up on my father because we wanted to eat like our friends and our American neighbors. We wanted TV dinners and the easy, fun packaged foods we saw advertised on TV and overwhelmingly present in the grocery aisles. Back then, one of my mother's favorite ways to cook included dumping a can of cream of mushroom soup on pork chops and baking it in the oven or pouring a package of sloppy job mix into a pan of ground beef. Our vegetables were out of a can or frozen, too. Of course, it's okay to use canned or frozen food on occasion (it's so convenient), but during my childhood, this was an everyday thing—the way people regularly made home-cooked meals. The four of us loved that particular period of our food history; it was our Americana phase.

My dad, however, couldn't stand it! He made his own food, roasting whole fish or chicken in the oven with garlic, cilantro, and chilies. He'd make steaming rice and pots of beans. Why would we (the new American eaters) want that when we could have mom's mushroom soup pork chop, or a TV dinner with that little apple pie? He even had a garden, where he grew his own tomatoes and herbs—and this was way before the urban garden thing became trendy.

As much as we loved our Americana fare, the novelty soon wore off. Over time, my mother stopped making packaged food, and my brothers and I started to like what my dad was cooking up. We even grew to love cilantro, despite screaming about it constantly because my father used to put it on *everything*.

If you haven't already figured this out, my family loves to eat. I mean, *really* loves to eat. To this day, every Sunday we get together at my mom's house and have dinner with my cousins, aunts, uncles, and grandma. Over the years, the tradition has grown to include new people almost weekly. Sometimes I invite a friend or two, or someone

else brings a friend, and it goes on from there. I'm lucky that, as much as we love to eat, most of us love to cook, as well. I took advantage of this to test many of the recipes in this book. My eleven-year-old niece even made many of these recipes herself. The food—these recipes—is simple. *Latin food is simple!*

Just like our beloved rice and beans. I can say with some certainty that if you grew up in a Latino household, you ate rice and beans. Even though the basic ingredients are the same, the variations are endless, and the little differences make every version unique.

This goes for empanadas, tortillas, and even flan, churros, and more. If you have churros in Mexico, they will probably be slightly different then the churros in Portugal, but I am sure every version will be delicious.

Across Latin America, the food and ingredients are similar and so is the warmth and hospitality of the people. They enjoy good food and good drink, and they want to share it with everyone. In Latin communities, it is common for someone you just met to invite you to a home-cooked meal with their family.

The recipes in this book demonstrate the way I cook for myself and my family, but also, most importantly, the way I cook in my restaurants. Growing up in Los Angeles, I've enjoyed foods from all over Latin America, and the indelible influences of these cultures—as well as my father's, mother's, grandmother's and aunts' cooking—is present in each dish. The food is simple, fresh, and healthy, and the recipes are easy to follow. Good food doesn't have to be complicated!

I hope you'll appreciate the healthy twist I've given the food of my childhood. These days, remarkably, salsa outsells ketchup. Today, Latin food is a part of American culture. I hope you'll enjoy this book as much as I've enjoyed the journey of creating it and conjuring recipes that blend so much of my childhood and that of my many and varied neighbors.

Good Food, Good Life!
—Isabel

Latin Table

For my first wedding, we decided to have a small ceremony at a church with a small group of family and friends and then a big reception the next day where we invited everyone. The day before the small ceremony, we changed our mind about going to a restaurant with the group (this was still about forty people) and decided last minute to have a dinner after the wedding ceremony at my parents' house. This meant my father had to throw together dinner for forty people on the fly. He prepared it lightning fast and was as calm as a cucumber the entire time. This dinner ended up being one of the most memorable meals of my life.

I know you want to know what he made, so here it is: Lechon Asado, black bean rice with sweet plantains, and a simple salad with tomatoes, red onion, and capers. He put everything on giant, colorful platters. It was a beautiful Latin Table. Our friends talked about this food for years. Everybody ended up dancing to salsa music all night and drinking Puerto Rican rum. That night is one of my fondest family, friend, and food memories.

This is what the Latin Table is all about. Latin food doesn't take a ton of planning; it's very basic and simple. It's about enjoying yourself with friends. It shouldn't be stressful to put together even if it's an impromptu meal.

Your Latin Kitchen Basics

We often gather together at my mother's house to cook, and she has a heck of a lot of stuff in her kitchen. She has two double-sided refrigerators, and they are always full to the brim—the freezers in both are full, too. In fact, I told her she's not allowed to buy anything else that would go in the freezer (except, of course, high-quality ice cream because we will always find a way to cram that in) until some of that stuff gets used or given away.

This also goes for the spices in her cupboards. You would think that, with all this foodstuff, when we go to cook at her house, she would have the most basic Latin ingredients on hand, right? Well, she doesn't. "What do you mean you don't have any cilantro, Ma?"

I made a list for her of all the things she should always have on hand. Since I had this list, I thought I would share it with you, too. This is *very* basic but provides a good start for you aspiring Latin cooks out there.

- A variety of salts. I could write a whole book on this, but my main rule is no table salt at all. At home I always have on hand sea salt, pink Himalayan salt, and I really like a nice flaked finishing salt. After that I am always experimenting with different fun salts. Keep in mind some salts taste saltier then others, so while experimenting with new salts and recipes it is always good to go with less at first and add more later, if necessary.
- Best quality extra virgin olive oil for sauces, salsas, finishings, etc.
- Good-quality olive oil for simple frying. *Yes, I use olive oil for frying.* I wouldn't fry chicken for a hundred people with it, but for frying on a very small scale, I think it tastes good. As long as you keep the oil between 350-375 degrees (use your deep - fry thermometer for this) it is okay to fry with olive oil.
- Coconut oil
- Chili flakes
- Ground cumin
- Ground chili (mild)
- Ground ancho chili and or ground chipotle chili (these two are both spicy)

- Chipotle chilies in adobo sauce
- Panko bread crumbs
- Red onion
- Garlic
- Tomatoes, best you can find
- Cilantro
- Jalapeños, both red and green
- Dried Guajillo chilies
- Short-grain brown rice
- Black beans, both dried and canned (in case you're in a time crunch)
- A bag of good-quality shrimp in the freezer (they thaw quick if someone stops by unexpectedly)

Since you got me going, let me list a few kitchenware items:

- A variety of mason jars with extra plastic lids, to store spices and sauces.
- Cast-iron pans. I love my cast-iron pans and I have just about every size and shape they make. They will last more than a lifetime and you can cook and serve with them.

- A deep-fry thermometer.
- Good knives. Good-quality knives are a real investment and one I totally encourage you to make. It spells the difference between a fun, easy time in the kitchen and a frustrating one. Also, if you take care of your knives, they can last for a lifetime.
- Blender or food processor. Handheld blenders also work well for sauces, in addition to being a great way to purée soups. Good blenders will work, too. A small food processor is also a great and inexpensive gadget.
- Cutting board. Most every budding cook has a cutting board. In addition to big wooden ones, I like to have a variety of small and large plastic ones. Having separate cutting boards for meat, poultry, and fish is a brilliant way to prevent contamination in your clean kitchen.

- Measuring cups and a good assortment of utensils. Most of you probably have these basic, necessary kitchen items. These are usually the first things we buy or the little gems we inherit when someone moves or gets better stuff. Every time you cook, you need to measure, stir, or whisk something or other and it'll be a lot easier if you have the proper tools.
- Rice cooker. I rely on the rice cooker to make perfect rice while I devote my attention to other parts of the meal. You can definitely make rice without one, but it is inexpensive, almost foolproof, easy to clean, and it saves me a ton of time in the kitchen.
- Salad spinner. Using the salad spinner is the easiest and gentlest way to clean your lettuce. Because the salad spinner is easy to clean and inexpensive, it is a great little gadget to have in the kitchen.
- Strainer. Besides the usual strainer business, I like to rinse my fresh veggies and then let them drain for a bit before putting them in the salad spinner.
- Small and medium saucepots, sauté pans, and a stockpot. It is wise to buy good-quality stove and ovenware. As with knives, good pots and pans can last a lifetime.
- Stand mixer.
- Graduated stainless steel bowls.
- Assortment of glass and metal bowls and baking pans.
- Kitchen scale.

Family, Friends, and Food

I feel blessed—I have a wonderful family and amazing friends. We thoroughly enjoy each other's company and centering our gatherings around food. We cook together, go to restaurants together, travel together, and shop together (for food!). If we plan a trip, you can bet a big part of it revolves around eating and cooking. Holidays and parties are taken seriously; planning and preparing could go on for weeks, even months, if the occasion is big enough.

Besides my family's Sunday dinners, once a year, all of us (Grandma, aunts, uncles, cousins, and always some friends) go to our family farm. We hike, swim, and go into the city and explore. What we enjoy the most is being able to go into the field and pick our produce; there is nothing like making chili rellenos with chilies you picked yourself earlier in the day or roasting freshly picked corn. Going to the local butcher for our meat and to the local fishermen for our seafood is all part of our routine.

Getting up early and making cowboy breakfasts outside, over an open fire, is one of our favorite things about this annual trip. Even the coffee tastes better when you make it outside. Dinners include big salads, chickens on the rotisserie, or fish over the grill.

This trip is about much more than just good food and a great family vacation, though. In the process, we are teaching our kids where our food comes from. The huge amount of time, effort, and hard work farming requires can't be truly appreciated unless you see it firsthand. I didn't have the chance to experience this until I was an adult. I grew up in Los Angeles; we thought our food came from big-box stores. I tell the same silly joke all the time—*Now that I know how hard farming is, I think a cucumber should cost $40.* Letting your kids plant seeds, take care of the plant, and then pull a carrot out of the ground creates a valuable lesson.

I also feel extremely lucky to live and work in San Diego. Besides being a beautiful place to live, this town has a tight-knit culinary community. We do events together, we go to restaurants together, we go on trips together. The culinary scene is exploding throughout Mexico; in San Diego we are so lucky to be able to drive to Tijuana or the amazing Valle de Guadalupe. Tijuana isn't just for tacos anymore; it is home to hipster food trucks, breweries, and outstanding restaurants. Valle de Guadalupe, Mexico's wine region, is unique and truly amazing with its fantastic resorts and world-class restaurants. Many of the restaurants in Valle have their own organic farms and outdoor kitchens where they cook over an open fire.

After my years of spending time with this remarkable chef community, that plays and travels together, I now know we share most of the same goals and beliefs: we want to live joyful lives doing what we love to do while respecting the planet and taking good care of its resources and doing our best to spread the good word.

Starters

This chapter is about fun food, feisty food, and yummy *little* bites (though some may not be so little). These starters don't have to be nibbles before the main course; these recipes really can hold their own. They can be the party!

You can pick three, four, or even five of these recipes, add a couple of cocktails, and you'll have a pretty snazzy soiree. How about Chipotle Chicken Wings, Roasted Cauliflower, and Plantain Fritters along with a pitcher of Blackberry Chili Margaritas? If you get really ambitious, add the Shrimp Cakes with Chipotle Mayo and Mezcaladas!

Roasted Cauliflower with Chili Flakes

SERVES 4

Cauliflower is the new it *vegetable. I don't know if there is another vegetable that restaurants are cutting into steaks and charging $19 for (I did actually see that on a menu). This recipe is especially good when you let the cauliflower get nice and caramelized.*

Olive oil
1 large cauliflower head, cleaned and sliced
    into cauliflower steaks
3 tablespoons butter, cubed
1 teaspoon red chili flakes
Salt

Heat oven to 375°F.

Drizzle generous coating of olive oil over a rimmed baking sheet or other ovenproof baking vessel. Arrange cauliflower steaks on desired vessel. Lay cubes of butter over cauliflower. Sprinkle with chili flakes and salt.

Bake until cauliflower is tender and a deep golden brown color, about 25 minutes.

Shrimp Cakes
with Orange Chili Oil Dressing

SERVES 4–6

These cakes are the real deal. They aren't loaded with breadcrumbs as a filler, so they are plump with shrimpy goodness. They can be made gluten-free if you omit the flour; just use 2 tablespoons to form shrimp cakes, then slowly slide the shrimp mixture into the pan. Personally, I like the bit of crispiness the light coating of flour adds.

If you're not a fan of Chili Oil, many sauces in the sauce chapter go well with these shrimp cakes, such as chipotle mayo or cilantro lime sauce. Or if you feel like a chunky salsa, try the chipotle corn salsa. My whole family loves these, and when I make them, they are gone in no time.

1 pound shelled deveined shrimp, chopped
¼ cup red onion, finely chopped
¼ cup cilantro, chopped, more to garnish
Salt

1 egg, beaten, more or less as needed
2 cups all-purpose flour, more as needed
Vegetable oil, for frying
Orange Chili Oil Dressing (page 97)

Transfer chopped shrimp, red onion, and cilantro to a mixing bowl. Lightly sprinkle with salt. Pour beaten egg over the other ingredients; the egg will help bind everything together. Gently mix.

Form shrimp mixture into chubby little cakes (this is messy but worth it). Have the flour ready to go on a plate and dip each shrimp cake. The shrimp mixture should be wet enough to hold everything together and to get the flour to stick. I gently toss the shrimp mixture from hand to hand to dust off some of the excess flour. The desired result would be for the patty to have just have a *light* coating of flour on the outside. You will need to gently press the patties together; don't expect them to hold together like Play-Doh. Once they are cooked, they will hold their shape. Continue making patties until all the shrimp is used.

In a large, straight-sided sauté pan, heat ¼ inch of oil over a medium-low flame until small bubbles form on the bottom. Cook cakes about 3 minutes each side or until golden brown and cooked through. If the cakes begin to brown too quickly, lower heat. Your desired finished shrimp patty should be a deep golden brown color. Transfer to paper towel–lined plate. Blot excess oil, transfer to serving platter, garnish with chopped cilantro, and serve with Orange Chili Oil Dressing.

Simple Ceviche
with Olive Salsa Fresca

To make a good ceviche, the key is to use the freshest fish possible. The smell test is the easiest way to tell if your fish is fresh; a clean, mild scent is what you are after. Never buy fish that smells fishy. Texture should be nice and firm with no gray tones in the coloring of the fish. The rest is easy-peasy. I serve this ceviche with a bowl of chimichurri sauce on the side; it makes this dish shine. It is well worth taking a few minutes to make it!

1 pound sea bass (halibut, snapper, or other
  firm-fleshed fish fillets will do as long as it's
  the freshest you can get your hands on),
  cut into ¼-inch dice
1¼ cups fresh lime juice or just enough to
  cover the fish
Salt
2 tablespoons olive oil
¼ cup red onion, small dice
1 Roma tomato, diced
¼ cup green olives, pitted and sliced
¼ cup kalamata olives, pitted and sliced
½ cup cilantro, chopped
1 avocado, diced
Chimichurri sauce (page 101)

In a large, preferably glass, bowl, toss fish with lime juice, cover, and refrigerate until the fish is cooked to your preference. This should take between 1 and 3 hours depending on how cooked you like your ceviche. During this time, give fish an occasional stir so it cooks evenly. When fish is cooked to your liking, discard lime juice. Sprinkle with salt, and drizzle with olive oil. Toss gently with remaining ingredients.

Serve with bowl of chimichurri, tortilla chips, or tostadas.

Queso Fundido, Three Ways

*No matter how large and diverse a dinner table I set for my parties, this queso fundido
is always the first thing finished!*

4 cups jack cheese, shredded, more as desired
Chipotle Corn Salsa (page 95)
Basic Salsa (page 93)
2 jalapeños, sliced, a combination of both red
    and green is nice
2 tablespoons green onion, chopped
2 or 3 cherry tomatoes, sliced, heirloom are
    great if available
Crispy Plantains (page 18), or good tortilla
    chips, or good tortillas to serve alongside

Preheat oven to 375°F.

Fill 3 small baking vessels (about 6 inch diameter) with about 1⅓ cup cheese (I use mini cast-iron pans). Top one vessel with about 2 tablespoons corn salsa (save remaining corn salsa to serve on the side with basic salsa). Fill the next vessel with sliced jalapeños, and the last vessel with chopped green onion and cherry tomato slices.

Bake in preheated oven until cheese is melted and bubbly. Serve alongside remaining corn salsa, basic salsa, and desired accompaniment of plantains, chips, or tortillas.

Crispy Plantains
with Heirloom Tomato Pico de Gallo
and Chipotle Cream

⁂

SERVES 4

My favorite customer is named Sebastian. He just turned five, and his favorite thing to eat is plantains. He loves them so much that he actually thinks the name of my restaurant is Plantains. He also loves the chipotle cream, and he isn't afraid to pull on a server's pant leg to ask for more!
These plantains are twice-fried; first to soften the flesh, and then, after a smash with a mallet or a small plate, they go back into the oil to fry to a golden crispness. Here I use them as a heartier replacement to chips.

2 green plantains
4 cups vegetable oil, for frying
Salt

Heirloom Tomato Pico de Gallo
  (page 105)
Chipotle Cream (page 100)

To peel plantains: Cut off each end and then cut in half. Use a paring knife to score the plantain in long, diagonal slits down the sides. Soak in warm water for 20 minutes, then peel the skin off in strips from top to bottom.

Cut each peeled plantain half into 4 pieces, cut on a diagonal. Submerge in salted water until ready to fry, at least 15 minutes. Drain and blot dry with paper towels.

In a large, straight-sided sauté pan, heat 2 inches of oil over a medium flame until small bubbles form on the bottom. Working in batches, transfer the plantain pieces to the hot oil and cook until lightly golden and tender, about 2 minutes.

Remove the slices from the oil to a paper towel–lined tray. Place them between 2 pieces of parchment paper and gently smash with a meat tenderizer or mallet or by pressing a small plate into the plantain. The resulting plantains should be about ¼-inch thick. If the plantain crumbles apart, it was not cooked enough. If the edges crumble, use the natural stickiness of the fruit to press it back together.

Raise the flame to medium-high and transfer the flattened plantains back to the pan. Cook them this time until golden brown on both sides, about 2 minutes. Transfer to paper towels to drain and sprinkle with salt.

When all of the plantains have been twice fried, arrange them on a serving platter. Serve with Heirloom Tomato Pico de Gallo and Chipotle Cream.

ABOUT PLANTAINS

A banana with a starchy nature, plantains are sometimes served as a savory part of the meal and, as they ripen and grow sweeter, occasionally make an appearance at dessert. Plantains have a tougher flesh and skin than bananas, with their skins ripening from green (the least ripe), to yellow, and then to black, which is when the plantain is at its sweetest.

Sopes with Baked Carnitas and Pickled Red Onion

I like to make sopes when my whole family gets together for our Sunday dinners. To make preparation easy, I form the sopes ahead of time and keep them between pieces of parchment paper. I cover them with plastic wrap and put a clean, damp towel on top so they stay moist. If you are planning on cooking them within a couple of hours of eating, it is fine to leave on the counter. If you prepare them any more than two hours prior, store in the refrigerator. Bring to room temperature before cooking. Then I just cook them off when it's time to eat.

Sopes are smaller and thicker than traditional tortillas and these sopes are cooked in a hot skillet rather than fried. Made with Masa Harina, a Mexican cornmeal flour, the toppings for sopes are endless: from grilled chicken to shrimp, steak, or carnitas, sopes are a great time to get creative with your favorite ingredients. Think of them as a blank canvas.

Masa Harina is available in Hispanic markets as well as many mainstream grocery stores.

1½ teaspoons ground cumin
1½ teaspoons ground chili powder
½ teaspoon dried Mexican oregano
¾ teaspoon salt
1½ pounds boneless pork shoulder, fat trimmed, cut into about 4 pieces
2 cups lager beer
About 2 cups Masa Harina
1 cup crumbled queso fresco
Pickled red onion (page 69)
Avocado sauce (page 101)
¼ cup cilantro leaves

Preheat oven to 300°F.

Combine the cumin, chili powder, oregano, and salt in a small bowl to make a seasoning mix. Cut pork into 4 pieces. Rub the seasoning on the pieces of pork and place the pork in a Pyrex casserole dish or other ovenproof baking vessel. Pour beer into baking vessel. Cover pork tight with aluminum foil. Bake in the preheated oven, and check after 1 hour for tenderness (take care when opening foil, the steam will be hot). The desired result is meat that is fork-tender. Continue cooking if necessary. When meat is tender, remove the foil, raise to 375°F, and bake until the carnitas is nicely browned, about 10 minutes. When meat has cooled enough to handle, shred carnitas into desired-size pieces.

While pork is cooking, place the masa harina and 1½ cups of water in the bowl of a stand mixer fitted with a paddle attachment. Mix on low to medium speed until incorporated and dough forms. Add 1 or 2 tablespoons of water or a little more masa (whichever is needed) to give the dough soft, Play-Doh-like consistency.

To make the sopes, pinch off pieces of dough to form golf ball-size spheres. Flatten them by passing back and forth between your hands to form tortillas that are 3 inches in diameter and ¼ inch thick. (This is the traditional way. I also like to put the dough between two pieces of parchment paper and then flatten with a plate.) Keep flattened sopes moist between pieces of parchment paper (each single row of sopes must be separated between another row of parchment paper). Place a clean, damp towel over the top layer of parchment paper until ready to cook.

Begin to cook sopes when carnitas are finished cooking. Heat a flat griddle or sauté pan over a medium flame. As a trial, place one sope on the hot surface. Cook until the sope begins to puff, turn, and cook the other side. Like pancakes, the first ones usually have to be thrown away as you gauge the cooking times. The sopes should be warm and soft all the way through.

Serve with bowls of the remaining ingredients for your guests to fill the sopes as they like.

Seared Ahi Tostadas with Avocado

SERVES 8

These tostadas are the perfect combination of easy, tasty, impressive, and hip. Use them for hot date material, or a small dinner party staple. There are three sauces listed with this recipe: Chipotle Mayo, Orange Chili Oil Dressing, and Isabel Sauce. You certainly don't need all three, I just had a hard time deciding which to list because they all go so well with the ahi! The Chipotle Mayo layers beautifully with the Orange Chili Oil Dressing and the Isabel Sauce is more like a little dribble of hot sauce.
As a party entree, having the extra sauces for your guests to choose from or to layer with adds fun to the table. Feel free to choose one, two, or all three of these sauces. If you have leftover sauce, believe me, you won't have trouble using them.
The ahi should be the freshest you can find, with a deep red color, firm and healthy texture, and good clean smell. Packaged prefried tostadas are sold in grocery stores and online, or you can make your own.

Vegetable oil, to coat pan
1 pound sushi grade tuna, cut into 1-inch-thick steaks
Chipotle Mayo (page 100)
Tostadas
1 avocado, each half thinly sliced
Orange Chili Oil Dressing (page 97) (optional)
Isabel Sauce (page 107) (optional)
Cilantro, chopped, to garnish

In a large, nonstick sauté pan, heat the oil over a medium-high flame. Sear the tuna steak for 30 seconds, turn, and sear the other side another 30 seconds (if you like your tuna cooked more, sear longer; alternatively, if you like it seared less, cook less). Transfer to a cutting board, and use a sharp, straight blade to cut the ahi into $\frac{1}{8}$-inch-thick slices. Cut across the grain.

Spoon and spread Chipotle Mayo on tostada and lay several pieces of tuna, followed by sliced avocado. Let guests top each tostada with a drizzle of Orange Chili Oil Dressing and/or Isabel Sauce and a sprinkle of cilantro.

Shrimp Salpicon

SERVES 6–8

This is great for a crowd and it's the kind of dish you can add to. If you have some extra pineapple in the fridge, chop it up, throw some in. Salted pepitas? Yep, those would be great as well. Jicama? Awesome. For me, this is what salpicon is about: throwing together all kinds of yummy stuff. There are many different versions of salpicon throughout Latin America from Mexico to Argentina. This is my version. (It's also another good example of how good layering sauces can taste and also how it can transform good recipes into great recipes.)

1 pound shrimp, peeled, deveined, poached
    until just done, and cut into bite-size pieces
½ pound Persian cucumbers, peeled and
    sliced into half circles
¼ red onion, thinly sliced
1-2 red jalapeños, sliced into thin circles
1 cup cherry tomatoes, cut in half or
    quartered, depending on size
½ cup cilantro, chopped
2 tablespoons lime juice
¼ cup olive oil
Salt
Cilantro Lime Sauce (page 106)
Isabel Sauce (page 107)

Gently toss first six ingredients together. In a small bowl, whisk together lime juice, olive oil, and then salt to taste. Drizzle olive oil mixture into the other ingredients, then give another gentle toss.

Serve with bowls of Cilantro Lime Sauce and Isabel Sauce for guests to drizzle as they please. Good-quality tortilla chips or tostadas are a great addition as well.

Baked Chipotle Chicken Wings

It's surprising how good these baked wings turn out with this really simple rub. Be generous when coating the wings. The oil from the pan adds flavor and will make it seem like they were fried, even though they're not! For the sauce, I add Louisiana hot sauce (FYI, I love Louisiana hot sauce) to give it that extra twang.

¼ cup mild chili powder
2 tablespoons ground cumin
1 tablespoon salt
3 pounds chicken wings, about
    25 winglets & drumettes
Olive oil, for coating

CHIPOTLE WING SAUCE
½ cup olive oil
3 chipotle chilies in adobo sauce
2 tablespoons brown sugar
¼ cup lime juice
1 cup Louisiana hot sauce

Preheat oven to 350°F.

Toss chili powder, cumin, and salt together to make a dry rub. Lightly drizzle the wings with olive oil and then sprinkle the wings thoroughly on all sides with the rub. You will most likely have some rub left over. Place wings on olive oil–coated baking pan (a large cast-iron pan works best) in one layer. If the wings are in one layer, the baking will create a crunchy, toasty skin that will combine with the flavorings of the rub. Bake for about 35 minutes.

If at this point the wings aren't crispy enough, raise the temperature to broil so the top layer of the wings get nice and crispy; it should take about 5 minutes to achieve this. As always, when using the broiler, keep a close watch so that the wings don't burn.

While wings are baking, purée ½ cup olive oil, chipotle chilies, brown sugar, and lime juice. Mix puréed chipotle sauce with 1 cup Louisiana hot sauce.

Serve wings hot with sauce on the side for guests to drench wings in as they please. Serve with sliced cucumbers and a side of Cotija Ranch Dressing (page 103).

Plantain Fritters

SERVES 4–6

These aranitas *are meant to look like "baby spiders," but they are simply crispy mounds of fried plantains. Serve them with Mango Mint Salsa (page 98) or give them the potato pancake treatment by topping them with a dollop of sour cream and a little caviar. As an appetizer or part of a main course, these are addictive.*

3 green plantains
Vegetable oil
Salt

Refer to page 19 to learn more about plantains, including how to cut them.

Blot the plantains dry after peeling. Grate the plantains using the large holes on a box grater. In a large, straight sided sauté pan, heat 2 inches of oil over medium flame. Make thin little patties of grated plantain; the starchiness of the plantains should be enough to hold the patties together. When small bubbles begin to form on the bottom of the pan, gently lay the patties into the hot oil (the oil should sizzle but not spatter, lower or raise the flame accordingly). Fry until the aranitas are crisp and golden brown, about 7 minutes, turning once. Transfer to a paper towel–lined tray to drain. Sprinkle with salt. These taste great with Chipotle Cream (page 100).

Salads, Soups & Sides

I really am a meat-and-potatoes person, or more accurately, a rice-bean-and-chicken person. So if I cook up a salad or soup, it's gotta be good. You can serve these salads with grilled fish or meat, and of course roasted or grilled chicken, making them a satisfying meal. Salad as main course is becoming more and more popular these days, but they're also great starters.

The soups in this chapter are simple and satisfying with interesting flavors. Try pairing one of the salads with one of the soups for a homey dinner. One great combination is the Mexican Ensalada Buena with Tomato Soup with Guajilo Chili. Stick around to the end of this chapter and you'll find some tasty side dishes as well.

Oven-Roasted Vegetable Salad with Sofrito Vinaigrette

SERVES 4–6

Sofrito has so many uses in Spanish cooking because of the depth it adds. A simple balsamic dressing is elevated to a new level. The oven-roasted vegetables give this salad some heft. Chargrilled shrimp or chicken can be added to boost this to main-course material.

3 Roma tomatoes, each cut into 4-6 wedges
1 large zucchini, split and cut into semicircles
1 large red bell pepper, seeds discarded, cut into thin strips
Salt
Pepper
2 tablespoons of olive oil + 3 additional tablespoons
¼ pound shitaki mushrooms, cleaned and sliced
2 tablespoons balsamic vinegar
3 cups mixed lettuce, rinsed and spun dry
Sofrito Vinaigrette (page 109)

Preheat the oven to 350°F.

Place the tomato wedges, zucchini, and red pepper on a baking sheet. Sprinkle with salt and pepper, then drizzle the vegetables with 2 tablespoons of olive oil. Slow roast in the oven for about 30 minutes. Set aside to cool.

While the vegetables are roasting, heat the remaining 3 tablespoons of olive oil in a sauté pan over a medium heat until hot. Add the mushrooms to the pan and drizzle with the balsamic vinegar. Cook the mushrooms for 2 minutes. The mushrooms should be soft and well browned. Set aside.

To serve, divide the lettuce among 4 plates. Arrange the grilled vegetables over the lettuce and drizzle the Sofrito Vinaigrette. Serve immediately.

ISABEL'S TIP
The vegetables are served at room temperature, so they can be made in advance, along with the Sofrito Vinaigrette.

Heirloom Tomato, Avocado, and
Cotija Cheese Salad

Heirloom Tomato, Avocado, and Cotija Cheese Salad with Roasted Tomato Vinaigrette

SERVES 4–6

The dressing makes this salad, and offering some nice, toasted bread to sop it up is a bonus. It is hearty enough to hold its own with a nice glass of red wine, or you can serve it as a side dish with something hearty like Grilled Ribeye Steak (page 85). It also pairs well with grilled or roasted chicken or fish.

2 heirloom tomatoes, cut into wedges
½ pint heirloom cherry tomatoes, cut in half or quartered
Finishing salt
¼ red onion, sliced thin

1 avocado, sliced
¼ cup cotija cheese, chunky crumble
Roasted pepitas (optional)
Cilantro, chopped, for garnish
Roasted Tomato Vinaigrette (page 99)

Arrange large heirloom tomato on serving platter followed by heirloom cherry tomatoes. Lightly sprinkle with finishing salt. Top with red onion and avocado slices, and sprinkle with cotija cheese, roasted pepitas, and chopped cilantro. Drizzle with a light coating of Roasted Tomato vinaigrette.

Corn and Avocado Chopped Salad

SERVES 4

This simple salad is a great little starter for Ropa Vieja (page 88) or as a chunky salsa.

4 ears of corn, kernels removed from the cobs
¼ red onion, diced
3 roma tomatoes, diced
½ cup cilantro, chopped
2 jalapeños, minced, seeds discarded

1 avocado, sliced in half, pit removed, peeled, and cut into chunks
¼ cup olive oil
3 tablespoons fresh squeezed lemon
Salt

Combine the corn, onion, tomatoes, cilantro, and minced jalapeño in a medium bowl. Toss to combine. Add the diced avocado. Give the olive oil and lemon a quick whisk and drizzle over salad. Mix gently, and sprinkle with salt to taste.

Mexican Ensalada Buena

This is another salad that can become a hearty meal with the addition of some grilled chicken, steak, shrimp, carnitas, or any other protein you wish. As you know by now, I like layering flavors, hence the two salad dressings. The Cumin Vinaigrette is refreshing and light while the Cotija Ranch is creamy and soooooooooo good.

Oil, for frying
2 soft corn tortillas, sliced into thin strips
Salt
1 head romaine hearts, leaves torn into
    bite-size pieces, rinsed, and spun dry
3/4 cup red cabbage, shredded
2 Persian cucumbers, scored and sliced into
    diagonal rounds
4 radishes, thinly sliced
1/4 cup pepitas
Chipotle Corn Salsa (page 95)
Cumin Vinaigrette (page 105)
Cotija Ranch Dressing (page 103)

In a straight-sided sauté pan, heat 2 inches of oil over a medium flame until small bubbles form on the bottom. Add tortilla strips, working in batches to make sure they are completely submerged. Fry until very crispy. Remove to a paper towel–lined plate to drain. Sprinkle with a bit of salt. Set aside until ready to plate salad.

In a large bowl, gently toss romaine hearts, cabbage, cucumbers, radishes, pepitas, and Chipotle Corn Salsa (save some Chipotle Corn Salsa and radish to garnish the top of the salad) with a light drizzle of the Cumin Vinaigrette. Garnish top of salad with remaining Chipotle Corn Salsa, radishes, tortilla strips, and chopped cilantro. Serve with a bowl of Cotija Ranch Dressing on the side for guests to dollop on their salads as they please.

Spanish Potato Salad

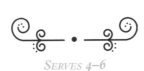

SERVES 4–6

Each of the potato salad recipes in this book are very different, but both are great side dishes, so that's why I had to include them both. This particular potato salad was my father's favorite.

3 pounds small, waxy, thin-skinned potatoes,
   such as new potatoes
2 cloves of garlic, peeled and sliced as thin as
   possible
½ cup olive oil
2 tomatoes, vine-ripened or Roma, cut in
   ¼-inch slices
¼ medium red onion, thinly sliced
3 tablespoons capers
2 lemons, halved
¼ cup cilantro leaves (optional, for garnish)
Salt

Place potatoes in a large pot and cover with salted water. Bring to a boil and cook until tender, 20 minutes.

Meanwhile, combine the garlic and the olive oil in a small saucepan. Heat over a medium flame, swirling the pan frequently to infuse the oil with the flavor of the garlic. The garlic will become soft and translucent, but it shouldn't begin to brown.

When the potatoes are done cooking, drain through a colander, let cool enough to handle, and slice in half. Spread the potato slices on a serving platter. Arrange the tomato and onion slices over the potatoes and then sprinkle the platter with capers.

Drizzle the warm olive oil over the platter. Squeeze the lemons over the platter and follow with a sprinkling of cilantro and salt (but keep in mind that capers are salty).

Potato Salad
with Bacon, Chives, and Cotija Ranch Dressing

SERVES 4

This potato salad is always a big hit at our family gatherings. It goes great with the Ribs with Chipotle BBQ Sauce (page 59) or the Brisket with Isabel Sauce (page 65). The Cotija Ranch Dressing is especially good and pulls it all together. The bold, contrasting flavors of the chives and the bacon are just what this creamy, tangy dressing needs to make a great potato salad anything but ordinary.

2 pounds red potatoes, scrubbed and cut in half
Cotija Ranch Dressing (page 103)
½ cup chives, sliced thin
½ pound bacon, cooked crispy, chopped

Place potatoes in a large pot and cover with salted water. Bring to a boil and cook until tender, about 25 minutes. Drain and cool, cut into ¼-inch slices.

Gently toss potatoes with generous amount of Cotija Ranch Dressing, half of the chopped chives, and half of the chopped bacon. Save the other halves to top off when plating.

Arrange on serving platter, drizzle more Cotija Ranch Dressing as desired, and sprinkle with remaining chives and chopped bacon.

Kale Salad
with Pineapple Jicama Salsa and Pepitas

SERVES 4

To say that kale rose in popularity in recent years is an understatement. I have to admit, many of my kale-salad-eating experiences were too chewy and too green-tasting (not in a good way). I wanted this to just be a good salad, and I think it is.

1 bunch lacinato kale, washed, tough ribs
    removed, chopped
Pineapple Jicama Salsa (page 96)

Minty Cilantro Dressing (page 100)
Roasted Salted Pepitas (page 128)

Place kale on serving platter and top with pineapple jicama salsa. Drizzle with Minty Cilantro dressing, and sprinkle with Roasted Salted Pepitas. Easy enough, right?

Citrus Salad
with Arugula and Tequila Honey Dressing

This is a refreshing and elegant salad that everyone will love. Tequila enhances these bright, citrusy flavors and adds a very Latin touch. For the less adventurous or (if this is even possible) people who don't like tequila, substitute the Tequila Honey Dressing for Orange Oregano Dressing or Cilantro Vinaigrette.

1 navel orange
1 pink grapefruit
1 blood orange
1 tangerine
3 cups baby arugula, washed and dried
¼ small red onion, thinly sliced
¼ cup cilantro, chopped
¼ cup fresh mint, chopped
Tequila Honey Dressing (page 104)
Finishing salt

Remove the peel, white pith, and seeds from the orange, grapefruit, blood orange, and tangerine and discard. Slice the citrus into ¼-inch rounds. On a large platter, lay arugula and top with all citrus, red onion, cilantro, and mint. Drizzle with Tequila Honey Dressing. Salt to taste.

Working with Citrus

My son, Robbie, is a chef and would segment the citrus for this salad. For non-cheffy folks, that might seem daunting. An easy way to cut the citrus is to slice off the top and bottom ends of the fruit. Place a flat end on a cutting board and, using a chef's knife, cut away the peel from top to bottom, removing as much of the white pith as possible. Slice into wheels and half wheels.

Cucumber Radish Salad
with Cilantro Lime Sauce

SERVES 4–6

The simplest of salads. Easy, light, crunchy, and bright, this is a great addition to any meal. You can use a single variety of cucumbers and radishes or you can mix and match. I recommend English, Persian, and Japanese cucumbers, and there are so many lovely types of radishes that you really can't go wrong no matter which you choose!

1 pound cucumbers, peeled and sliced on the diagonal
1 bunch radishes, trimmed and sliced

Cilantro Lime Sauce (page 106)
½ cup cilantro, washed and chopped

Arrange cucumbers on a platter and top with radishes, drizzle with Cilantro Lime Sauce, and garnish with chopped cilantro.

Sautéed Kale
with Rainbow Peppers

SERVES 4–6

This is often a popular special at my restaurants, where we even serve this as a breakfast item with the addition of eggs and tomatillo sauce. I recommend using lacinato kale for this recipe; it tastes great when you crisp it up a little bit around the edges and sprinkle it with good salt.

2 tablespoons olive oil + more as needed
½ red onion, sliced
1 red bell pepper, sliced, seeds and ribs removed

1 yellow bell pepper, sliced, seeds and ribs removed
1 bunch kale, rinsed, center rib removed, leaves rolled and sliced
Salt

Heat 2 tablespoons of olive oil in a large sauté pan over a medium flame. When the oil is hot, add the onion and bell peppers. Cook until vegetables are cooked through and have some slightly charred edges. Set onion and pepper mix aside. Add the kale to the pan and sauté until tender, about 4 minutes. Return bell pepper/onion mix to pan (save a third of the bell pepper/onion mix to top off kale because it looks pretty), give a couple of quick stirs, season with salt, and serve.

*Heirloom Carrot Ribbons
with Cumin Vinaigrette*

Heirloom Carrot Ribbons with Cumin Vinaigrette

SERVES 4–6

This salad is a beauty and anyone can do it with a decent peeler—the kind hipster bartenders use to make pretty citrus garnishes for cocktails. The rest of the ingredients are super simple as well.

1 bunch heirloom carrots, peeled into long ribbons
¼ small red onion, sliced thin
½ cup cilantro, chopped
1-2 Fresno chilies, sliced into thin circles

¾ cup queso fresco
¼ cup golden raisins
Cumin Vinaigrette (page 105)
4 large romaine lettuce leaves, gently torn

In a large bowl, gently toss together first six ingredients with a light drizzle of Cumin Vinaigrette. Arrange romaine lettuce leaves on a large platter or low-sided serving bowl, top with carrot ribbon salad mix, and serve with remaining dressing on the side for guests to drizzle as they wish.

Mango, Jicama, and Watermelon Salad with Hibiscus Syrup and Minty Cilantro Dressing

SERVES 6

We make this salad as a starter for family gatherings at the house. I put the dressing, chilies, cilantro, and tajin on the side so we don't intimidate the little ones. This blend of ingredients is Latin in spirit: fruity and vibrant. The two sauces are very pretty together and marry well with this fun, fruity salad.

1 large mango, peeled, pitted, and cut into spheres
1 jicama, peeled, cut into ½-inch matchsticks
1 (2-pound) seedless watermelon, rind removed, cut into ½-inch sticks

Hibiscus Syrup (page 103)
Minty Cilantro Dressing (page 100)
1 serrano chili, cut into thin circles
½ cup cilantro, chopped
Tajin (optional)

Arrange the mango, jicama, and watermelon on a platter. Drizzle with Minty Cilantro Dressing followed by a light drizzle of Hibiscus Syrup. Garnish with the serrano chili and cilantro. Sprinkle with tajin.

Tomato Soup with Guajilo Chili

SERVES 8

This was our house soup at one of my restaurants. Today, it's still one of my favorite soups to make at home. The toppings take this soup to the next level and make it fun for everyone.

1 pound Roma tomatoes
3 corn tortillas
Olive oil
1 yellow onion, peeled and diced
3 cloves of garlic, peeled and minced
3 carrots, diced
3 stalks of celery, diced
4 cups chicken stock

1 cup guajillo sauce
Salt
Cilantro Lime Sauce (page 106)
2 tortillas cut thin, fried, for garnish (optional)
Queso fresco, crumbled
1 avocado, sliced

Preheat broiler, place tomatoes on a rimmed baking sheet, and let broil until they begin to blacken. Use tongs to turn until all sides are charred. Transfer to a plate and let roasted tomatoes cool slightly. Heat corn tortillas over open burner until soft and then tear into pieces. Set aside tortillas with tomatoes.

Heat 2 tablespoons oil in heavy-bottomed stockpot. Add onion, garlic, carrots, and celery. Sauté until onion begins to turn translucent and carrots are tender, about 8 minutes. Take care to stir mixture as it sautés to avoid burning the garlic. Join onion mixture with tomatoes/tortillas in blender and purée until mixture has a nice, slightly thick and smooth consistency. Place mixture back in stockpot and add 4 cups of chicken broth (more or less, depending on your desired thickness). Add guajillo sauce to pot, stir all ingredients together, and simmer 20 minutes to let flavors meld. Salt to taste.

To garnish, add Cilantro Lime Sauce, fried tortilla strips, queso fresco, and avocado.

Chicken and Potato Soup with Coconut Milk

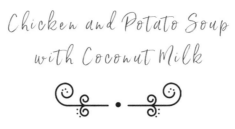

SERVES 6

This is as simple and restorative as chicken soup is meant to be, with a twist! It's an adaptation of my Spanish grandmother's chicken soup. My recipe calls for coconut milk; Mamma's version used more garlic and olive oil and skipped the coconut milk. This soup doesn't require stock or cream. Instead, its richness comes from potatoes, coconut milk, and puréeing ingredients together.

1 pound russet potatoes, peeled and cut into
   1-inch pieces (about 3 cups)
1 yellow onion, peeled and diced (about 1 cup)
2 carrots, peeled and diced (about 1 cup)
3 cloves garlic, smashed, skins discarded
2 boneless, skinless chicken breasts halves or
   1 whole breast, cut into 2-inch pieces
2 cans coconut milk (not low fat)
Salt

Place the potatoes, onion, carrots, garlic, and chicken breasts in a heavy-bottomed stockpot. Add cold water to cover the ingredients. Bring to a boil and then reduce to a simmer. Cook until the potatoes are tender and the chicken breast is cooked, about 30 minutes.

Remove from heat and strain the solids from the broth, reserving both separately. Working in batches, place the solids, including the chicken, in a blender and pulse the ingredients along with some of the reserved cooking liquid. Take care not to add too much of the cooking liquid, as you will be adding 2 cans of coconut milk later. You can always add more of the liquid at the end, but if you dump it in now, you can't take it away.

Repeat until all solids are puréed. Stir in 2 cans of coconut milk. Simmer on low to let the flavors blend. If you desire a thinner consistency, add more of the reserved cooking liquid. Add salt to taste.

Cocido

SERVES 8

Traditional Cocido is a staple of Latin cooking. In Spain, Portugal, and Mexico, it's called Cocido, and in Puerto Rico we have a similar version called Sancocho. Regardless of the name, its variations have been the basic meal in a pot for Latin people for hundreds of years. Everyone fights for the corn cob wheels that rest in this savory broth. Top each bowl with minced fresh mint and chopped red onion to add a bright finish.

3 tablespoons olive oil
1 yellow onion, peeled and chopped (1 cup +
    some for garnish)
6 cloves garlic, minced
1 beef shank, about 2 pounds
8 cups beef broth
2 bay leaves
2 ears corn, husked, and each cut into about
    6 wheels
2 carrots, sliced into ¼-inch discs
½ pound green beans
1 medium zucchini, diced
Salt and pepper, to taste
Fresh mint, for garnish

Heat the olive oil in a stockpot over a medium-high flame. Add the onion and garlic and cook until translucent, about 3 minutes. Remove with a slotted spoon and set aside. Add the beef shank to the pot and sear the meat undisturbed for about 3 minutes before turning and browning the other side. Return the onion and garlic to the pot, then add the broth slowly, using a wooden spoon to scrape the caramelized bits from the bottom of the pot.

Add the bay leaves and bring to a low simmer. Cook for 30 minutes, skim, and add the corn wheels. Continue to cook for 15 minutes and then add the carrots, green beans, and zucchini. Continue to cook until the vegetables are tender, about 30 minutes more.

Remove the shank from the pot, scrape all the meat from the bones, and cut into bite-size pieces. Return the meat to the broth and discard the bone. Season to taste with salt and pepper.

Serve the soup with a sprinkling of chopped raw onion and some fresh mint.

Chicken & Vegetables
with Chimichurri

SERVES 6

An alternate title for this recipe would be Bowl of Health! Simple soups like this one are just so nurturing! The Chimichurri adds just what it needs to make it snazzy. This soup is great with some crusty bread to dip in the leftovers.

3 tablespoons olive oil
1 yellow onion, peeled and diced (1 cup)
6 cloves garlic, minced
2 carrots, peeled and cut crosswise into
    ½-inch pieces
2 large or 3 medium celery stalks, cut into
    ½-inch pieces
2 bay leaves
6 cups chicken broth
1 medium zucchini, diced
2 (8-ounce) cooked boneless skinless chicken
    breast halves, shredded or cut into 1-inch
    pieces
Chimichurri Sauce (page 101)

Heat the olive oil in a stockpot over a medium-high flame. Add the onion, garlic, carrots, and celery and cook until onion is almost translucent, about 3 minutes.

Add the bay leaves, 6 cups of stock, and zucchini, and bring to a low simmer. Cook about 20 minutes or until vegetables are just cooked. Add shredded chicken breast and heat through. Drizzle with Chimichurri sauce right before serving, using any leftover chimichirri sauce to dip bread in.

Turkey Albondigas

Italians are famous for meatballs, but they play a big part in Latin cuisine as well. Most people I know who've traveled to Latin America return with a craving for albondigas, or meatballs. I use ground turkey for my meatballs rather than the traditional beef or pork recipes. This broth simmers briefly so the flavor is light and fresh, with just a touch of mint and diced red onion.

FOR THE MEATBALLS:

1 pound ground turkey, preferably white meat
2 cloves garlic
½ yellow onion, minced
2 tablespoons fresh mint leaves, finely chopped
1 egg
½ cup breadcrumbs, preferably homemade
1 teaspoon salt
¼ cup vegetable oil, for frying
½ cup flour, for dredging

FOR THE BROTH:

2 tablespoons tomato paste
2 chipotle chilies in adobo
3 tablespoons olive oil
1 yellow onion, peeled and diced
5 cloves garlic, peeled and minced
3 carrots, diced
2 celery stalks, diced
1 medium zucchini, diced
1 cup white wine
8 cups chicken stock
Fresh mint, chopped, for garnish

Combine the first 7 meatball ingredients in a medium mixing bowl. Use your hands to lightly form small meatballs, about 1 inch in diameter. Set the meatballs on a platter, cover with plastic wrap, and refrigerate until ready to cook. This can be done up to 1 day in advance.

For the broth, combine the tomato paste and chilies in a blender or food processor. Pulse and set aside.

Heat olive oil in a stockpot over a medium-high flame. Add the onion and garlic and cook until soft and translucent, about 3 minutes. Add the carrots, celery, and zucchini. Continue cooking for a few minutes more, stirring well to coat the vegetables with the olive oil. Add the white wine and simmer for 5 minutes. Stir in the tomato/chipotle mixture. Add the chicken stock and simmer until the vegetables are tender, about 20 minutes.

While the stock is simmering, lightly coat the meatballs with the flour. Heat the vegetable oil in a large sauté pan over a medium flame. Add the meatballs in batches until cooked through, about 5 minutes. When the meatballs have browned, transfer the cooked meatballs into the simmering broth. Remove the pot from the heat. Serve the soup steaming hot, topped with a sprinkling of chopped mint.

QUICK HOMEMADE BREADCRUMBS

Pulse 4 slices of hearty white bread in a food processor and pulse to a fine crumb.

Sweet Plantains

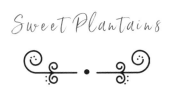

The skins of the plantains let you know how sweet they are, and this is a recipe for the ripest ones—those with yellow skins with black spots. When you see that, you know that the flavor of the plantain has turned sweet and the flesh still has structure. Unlike green plantains, you don't need to soak these before peeling them.

2 large plantains, yellow skins with black
    spots
Vegetable oil
Kosher salt

Cut each plantain into ½-inch slices.

Heat the oil in a large, deep-sided sauté pan over a medium-high flame. When small bubbles form on the bottom of the pan, place half the plantain slices into the hot oil (the oil should sizzle but not spatter, so lower or raise the flame accordingly). Fry for 1 minute before turning the slices over with a slotted spoon. Continue to cook for 1½ minutes more, until golden brown. Transfer to a paper towel–lined tray to drain. Sprinkle with kosher salt. Repeat with remaining plantain slices. Serve immediately.

To Peel the Plantains
Cut off each end and then cut the plantain in half. Use a paring knife to peel the skin off in strips from top to bottom.

Black Beans

As the main source of protein for most of the world's cuisines, beans play a major nutritional role. Nowhere is this more true than in Latin cuisine. Canned beans are convenient, and, best of all, fast—they can be on the table in minutes. When I haven't got time for dried, I used canned beans, enhanced with my own seasonings. They are equally delicious.

3 tablespoons olive oil
1 Spanish onion, diced (1 cup)
5 cloves garlic, peeled and minced
2 bay leaves
2 tablespoons cumin powder

2 tablespoons oregano
2 tablespoons chili powder
1 tablespoon dried sweet basil
1 pound dried black beans, picked over
    and rinsed

Heat the olive oil in a heavy-bottomed pot over a medium-high flame. Add the onion and garlic and cook until soft and translucent, about 3 minutes.

Add the bay leaves, cumin, oregano, chili powder, and basil. Stir to combine and cook 1 minute more. Add the beans and 10 cups of water. Bring to a boil, and then reduce heat to maintain a simmer. There should always be at least ½ inch of water above the beans, so add more if necessary.

Cook the beans until tender and creamy (2 to 2½ hours). Taste them to determine when they're done and, based on personal preference, how thick or soupy they should be.

Quick Black Beans

2 tablespoons olive oil
1 yellow onion, diced
5 cloves garlic, peeled and minced
1 tablespoon cumin
1 tablespoon chili powder

2 (14-16 ounce) cans black beans, rinsed
    in a colander
2 bay leaves
1 teaspoon dried oregano
1 teaspoon dried sweet basil
1 teaspoon salt

Heat the olive oil in a stockpot over a medium flame until hot. Add the onion and garlic and cook until soft and translucent, about 3 minutes. Add cumin and chili powder, stir to combine, and cook for 2 minutes more. Add the canned beans and 2 cups of water, bay leaves, oregano, sweet basil, and salt. Bring to a simmer and cook until the beans are thoroughly heated, 4 to 5 minutes.

Roasted Heirloom Carrots

I never knew I liked carrots this much! This makes such a pretty side dish and you can whip them up in no time. They're pretty delicious as well!

1 bunch large heirloom carrots, washed and
    sliced vertically down the middle
2 tablespoons olive oil + more to coat pan
1 teaspoon cumin powder
Finishing salt

Preheat oven to 375°F. Toss carrots with 2 tablespoons olive oil and lightly coat baking sheet with olive oil. Lay carrots on baking sheet. Sprinkle carrots with cumin powder. Bake until carrots have slightly shrunk in size and are beginning to caramelize, about 20 minutes. Transfer to serving platter and sprinkle with finishing salt.

Grilled Corn
with Jalapeño Honey Butter
and Cotija Cheese

The Jalapeño Honey Butter and cotija cheese combo are a great match. If you don't have a grill, just boil the corn for a few minutes and this recipe will still be a treat. If you have fresh sweet corn, the cooking time should be minimal.

6 ears corn, husked and shucked, but leave
    the core at the end
Jalapeño Honey Butter (page 109)
3/4 cup cotija cheese, crumbled
1/4 cup cilantro, chopped

On a medium-hot charcoal grill, gas grill, or cast-iron griddle pan, grill corn on all sides until char marks appear and corn is evenly heated, about 5 minutes. Slather corn with Jalapeño Honey Butter and sprinkle with cotija cheese, followed by chopped cilantro.

Oven-Roasted Sweet Potatoes with Cinnamon and Chili

SERVES 6

Cooking and serving in the same vessel is always a plus. Here is another time where I think a cast-iron pan is perfect. It's a crowd-pleaser even for the hungry men in my life because it's heartier then most vegetable sides.

1½ pounds baby sweet potatoes (or use
    large ones and cut after boiling)
Salt
Olive oil
3 tablespoons brown sugar
1 tablespoon cinnamon
2 tablespoons chili powder
1 tablespoon cumin
3 tablespoons butter

Rinse the sweet potatoes. Place in a large pot and cover with water. Add 1 teaspoon of salt and bring to a boil over a high flame. Cook until the potatoes are tender (pierce them with the tip of a paring knife), about 45 minutes. Drain and let cool.

Heat the olive oil in a large sauté pan (preferably cast iron) over a medium-high flame. Sprinkle the sweet potatoes with salt. When the oil is hot but not smoking, smash the sweet potatoes in the pan.

Toss the brown sugar, cinnamon, chili powder, and cumin together. Sprinkle over the top of the sweet potatoes and let it seep through any gaps in the smashed sweet potatoes. Put butter on top of sweet potatoes, in the crevices, and all over.

Transfer to a 375°F oven. Bake until the brown sugar melts and caramelizes.

Mains

Latin Americans love to entertain and feed people. When it comes to the main course, we don't mess around. Roasted or grilled meats, ceviches, whole chickens accompanied by flavorful beans, rice, or potatoes, and always with flavorful sauces or salsas. While Latin American countries are quite different and diverse, the cuisines have many similarities.

I am enamored with the burst of flavors Latin American cuisine offers. As bold and satisfying as it is, it can also be healthy. I believe that's because it is so simple and also because most Latin American cooks make their food from scratch.

Cumin Panko Chicken Empanizado

Empanizado is the Spanish word for "covered in breadcrumbs." A girlfriend of mine from Spain used to make the most delicious sandwiches with pollo empanizado. She put the breaded chicken on a soft roll with mayonnaise on one side of the bread and tomatoes that had a little garlic and olive oil on the other side. I loved this sandwich. Now, I make my own chicken empanizado with panko breadcrumbs and cumin, and I serve this as a dinner entrée instead of a sandwich. I serve it with sliced tomatoes with olive oil and capers and some boiled potatoes, capturing the same flavors my friend's sandwich featured.

4 boneless skinless chicken breasts, pounded to a ½-inch thickness
2 tablespoons ground cumin
2 teaspoons salt
Vegetable oil

1 cup flour
2 eggs, lightly beaten
1 (16-ounce) bag panko
1 lemon, cut into wedges

Use a mallet to pound the chicken breasts to a ½-inch thickness. If making a sandwich, pound more for a thinner cutlet. Place the chicken between 2 sheets of plastic wrap before pounding to keep things neat.

Combine the panko, cumin, and salt in a shallow bowl.

Heat ¼ inch oil in a large, straight-sided sauté pan over medium heat until small bubbles appear on the bottom of the pan.

Dredge the chicken breasts lightly in the flour, then the egg, and then the seasoned panko.

Place the chicken breasts in the sauté pan and cook for about 4 minutes per side. The chicken should be crisp and golden and cooked through. Transfer the chicken to a paper towel–lined tray. Transfer to serving plates and serve with a lemon wedge.

PANKO

Panko breadcrumbs are Japanese breadcrumbs that are slightly larger than regular breadcrumbs, with ragged edges. This means they are particularly appealing for frying—they absorb less oil and turn the best shade of golden brown. Used for tempura, these breadcrumbs produce a crisp and cleanly fried chicken breast. These days, you can find them at most supermarkets.

Ribs
with Chipotle BBQ Sauce

SERVES 8

When making these ribs for our family dinners, I use a mild chili powder so even our youngest, Ava, gobbles them up. Even though she doesn't like spicy food at all, this Chipotle BBQ sauce has expanded her horizons.

Removing the membrane from the back of the ribs is supposed to make the ribs tender. I am always too lazy to try that, and my ribs are still fall apart and are tender. For me, it's about cooking them low and slooooooooow. If you happen to have any leftovers (you probably won't), this meat can be used later to make mouthwatering tacos—just add some queso fresco and pickled onion.

Baby back pork ribs (about 5½ pounds)
¾ cup mild chili powder
¼ cup ground cumin
2 tablespoons salt
2 cans beer

Chipotle BBQ Sauce
6 chipotle chilies in adobo sauce
½ cup ketchup
2 tablespoons white vinegar
2 tablespoons brown sugar
2 tablespoons blackstrap molasses

To make BBQ sauce, purée all sauce ingredients.

Preheat oven to 300°F. Rinse and pat ribs dry. This is where you can remove the thin membrane from the back of the ribs if you wish to do so.

Toss the chili powder, cumin, and salt together. Rub generously all over the ribs. Reserve any leftover rub to reapply if desired. Arrange the ribs in an extra-large ovenproof pan with sides (you will probably need two pans). Pour beer into pan, cover tightly with extra thick aluminum foil, and crimp side of the pan tightly with foil.

Let ribs cook for 2 hours before checking. When checking, take care not to burn yourself—the steam will be hot. If ribs aren't yet super tender, cook for another 30 to 60 minutes.

Serve ribs with Chipotle BBQ Sauce on the side. This main goes great with Potato Salad with Bacon, Chives, and Cotija Ranch Dressing (page 37) and grilled corn with Jalapeño Honey Butter (page 109).

Shrimp Boil Latina Style

When you have a crowd to feed, this is the way to go. With one large pot, you can easily create a fun and flavorful meal for the whole group. For this recipe, I used both shell-on and shelled shrimp 20/25 count. The reason: shell-off shrimp get buttery and plump and are easier to eat, but the shell-on shrimp add extra flavor. Keep in mind that any good-quality shrimp will do. I don't usually suggest using frozen fish, but frozen shrimp have gotten really good and are so easy to prepare. If you keep a bag or two of shrimp in the freezer, this is a really easy recipe to make last minute. If you have the time, feel free to experiment with other seafood, clams, crab, etc.

2 bottles light beer

2 tablespoons ancho chili powder

1 tablespoon cumin powder

4 chipotle chilies in adobo sauce, minced

2 heads garlic, halved

2 red onion, halved

2 lemons, halved, seeds removed

2 pounds baby red potatoes, halved

1 pound spicy Spanish chorizo, cut into diagonal pieces (optional)

4 ears corn on the cob, shucked and halved

1 pound shrimp, shell on

1 pound shrimp, peeled, deveined, tail off

Salt

1 bunch cilantro, chopped

Jalapeño Honey Butter (page 109)

Limes, quartered (optional)

Crusty bread

Fill a very large, heavy-bottomed stockpot with 10 cups of cold water. You can add more water later if you feel it getting too crowded with the ingredients you will be adding. I try to keep it to the 10 cups water even if it starts getting a bit crowded, because it makes a really flavorful broth.

Add the first seven ingredients and bring to a boil. Add potatoes and chorizo, and reduce heat to a low simmer. Cook about 20 minutes or until potatoes are tender enough to pierce with a fork but not totally soft (remember: they will continue to cook). Add corn and cook another 5 minutes. Turn off heat and add shell-on shrimp first; stir in and submerge. When shrimp is barely starting to turn pink, add peeled shrimp and stir into other ingredients. Within 5 minutes, although heat is off, shrimp should be cooked through. If not, turn on the heat for a few minutes more, but take care not to overcook the shrimp. Add salt to taste.

Serve in pot or transfer to a serving vessel with a good amount of the cooking liquid. Garnish with chopped cilantro and lime quarters.

Melt half of the jalapeño butter to serve alongside the boil as a drizzle. Serve the other half of the jalapeño butter with crusty bread for the ultimate dipping vehicle for the broth!

Roasted Chicken Espanola

The Spanish are famous for great roasted chickens, with crisp, caramelized skin and flavorful juicy meat. I believe the best way to achieve this is with a simple dry salt brine, and by making sure your chicken gets a nice golden brown skin during the first part of baking. Spanish smoked paprika, rosemary, and thyme are all much-used spices in Spain, hence the name Roasted Chicken Espanola.

1 whole, free-range or organic chicken	2 tablespoons fresh rosemary, removed from stems, washed, and chopped
Salt	
1 tablespoon Spanish smoked paprika	1 tablespoon fresh thyme, removed from stems, washed, and chopped

Preheat oven to 425°F. Dry chicken with a paper towel. (A drier chicken makes for crispier skin.) Rub the chicken with a generous amount of salt inside and out. Use about ½ tablespoon salt per pound of chicken. Cover chicken loosely with plastic wrap and leave chicken in the fridge 1 to 2 days. I have gotten the best results by letting the chicken salt for 2 days.

When ready to roast, remove chicken from refrigerator, let come to room temperature, and discard any liquid. Sprinkle with paprika and toss rosemary and thyme together. Sprinkle rosemary-thyme mix all over chicken, inside the cavity, and under the skin. Place chicken in a heavy-duty roasting pan; my choice would be a cast-iron pan. If your cast-iron pan is seasoned, there is no need to oil the pan; if using another type of pan, a light coating of oil or cooking spray is advisable so your chicken doesn't stick. Roast chicken breast-side down for about 20 minutes. The skin should develop a nice golden-brown color within that time. If it doesn't, let it cook a bit longer before turning. It is important to get a crispy skin started before turning the chicken. When flipping the bird over, I use a sturdy metal spatula to pry the chicken from the pan (do this with care so you don't tear away the skin). A wooden spoon or tongs in the cavity is also helpful when flipping the bird. Cook another 20 minutes, more or less, to get the golden brown skin on the other side.

After the chicken is golden brown all over I lower the heat to 300°F. It should take about 10 minutes more to finish cooking, depending on your oven and the size of your bird. Chicken is cooked when the juices run clear and the drumsticks move easily (the internal temperature of the bird should be 160°F).

I would serve this chicken with simple roasted or boiled new potatoes. After chicken is carved, place the potatoes and the roasted chicken back in the pan to soak up all the drippings.

Halibut
with Roasted Tomato and Olive Caper Salsa

SERVES 4

This is one of those great dishes: easy to prepare with awesome results. The sauce is the secret with its deep tomato flavor and salty capers. A drizzle of cilantro sauce at the end gives the dish a bright-green finish.

4 Roma tomatoes, each sliced into 6
    wedges, and the wedges cut in half
Olive oil
Salt

4 (6-ounce) skinless halibut fillets
Cilantro Lime Sauce (page 102)
Olive and Caper Salsa Cruda (page 95)

Preheat oven to 350°F. Place tomatoes on a baking tray, drizzle lightly with olive oil, and season with salt. Roast in oven until the tomatoes appear shrunken and brighter in color, about 30 minutes. Set aside to cool.

Heat 2 tablespoons of olive oil in a 9-inch sauté pan. Dry the halibut with paper towels and season lightly on both sides with salt.

Place the halibut fillets in the hot pan and cook, undisturbed, for 2 minutes each side or until the fish has a golden-brown crust. Finish halibut in the oven until just done.

Drizzle a pool of Cilantro Lime Sauce on each plate. Place halibut fillets on the sauce and top with roasted tomatoes and Olive Caper Salsa Cruda.

Black Bean Rice with Sweet Plantains

SERVES 4

To put my own twist on the Latin American staple of black beans and rice, I always make mine with short-grain brown rice, which happens to be my favorite. The addition of sweet plantains gives this dish an awesome savory-sweet combination.

5 cups short-grain brown rice, cooked
3 cups black beans, cooked (page 50)
Olive oil
2 Roma tomatoes, diced
½ cup green onion, chopped

Chili Cumin Rub (page 110)
Sweet Plantains (page 49)
1 avocado, sliced
Cilantro, chopped
Salt

Let rice and beans come to room temperature. Gradually heat a large cast-iron pan until medium hot. Coat with a generous amount of olive oil, and add tomatoes and green onion. Top with a layer of brown rice. Sprinkle with the Chili Powder Cumin Rub (how much is really a personal choice; I like a lot of it). Stir a bit, add drained black beans on top of rice, and stir again to heat all ingredients together. Add more olive oil as desired.

Serve with Sweet Plantains and avocado slices, and garnish with chopped cilantro. You can also serve with Basic Salsa (page 93) or Isabel Sauce (page 107).

Baked Shrimp Diablo

SERVES 4

This is the perfect dish to make when you have a million other things to do. I serve it with a nice rice to soak up the sauce. Sautéed Kale with Rainbow Peppers (page 39) goes great with this.

⅓ cup olive oil
¾ cup Dijon mustard (spicy brown works, too)
Juice of 2 lemons (about ⅓ cup)

2 tablespoons chili flakes
1½ pounds large shrimp, peeled and deveined

Preheat oven to 375°F.

Whisk first four ingredients together. Pour over shrimp and gently stir to coat. Transfer shrimp to an ovenproof pan—a glass Pyrex baking dish works great. Bake shrimp until bubbly and cooked through, about 20 minutes.

Brisket with Isabel Sauce

SERVES 6

I am a firm believer in the sear. A nice, even caramelly sear adds so much flavor to this meat. I also don't trim the fat; when slow cooking, as we do here, most of the fat just melts into the meat, making it moist and flavorful. I suggest serving this brisket with Corn with Jalapeño Honey Butter and Potato Salad with Cotija Ranch. Make these recipes while your brisket is cooking.

Vegetable oil
4 pounds beef brisket
Salt
1 can lager beer
Isabel Sauce (page 107)

Preheat oven to 325°F.

In a large frying pan, heat 3 tablespoons of oil to high. Season both sides of the brisket with salt. Place brisket in pan and sear on medium-high until thoroughly browned, about 5 minutes per side.

Transfer brisket to baking vessel. Add beer to pan. Drizzle Isabel Sauce over brisket. Cover pan tightly with heavy-duty aluminum foil. Cook for 2 hours. At this point, check brisket for doneness. I like my brisket fork-tender, so I usually let mine cook closer to 2½ hours. Ovens vary, so take care not to dry out the brisket. If you have any leftover, this makes bomb tacos.

Pepita-Crusted Sea Bass
with Coconut Chili Oil

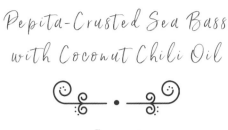

Class up your table with this dish! The coconut chili oil is a bold sauce and is the star of the show here. As always, buy the freshest fish available for the best results. Adding Kale Salad with Pineapple Jicama Salsa and Pepitas (page 37) creates a perfect combination for this meal.

½ cup roasted pumpkin seeds
½ cup roasted sunflower seeds
1 teaspoon salt (coarse salt works best here)
4 (6-ounce) sea bass fillets, skin removed
Olive oil
Coconut Chili Oil (page 97)

Pulse pumpkin seeds, sunflower seeds, and salt in blender or food processor. I like a nutty texture, so I don't pulse too long. The longer you pulse, the closer you'll get to a powder, which you don't want. Place pepita salt mix in a shallow dish. Rub the sea bass with oil, dredge the fillets in the pepita-salt mix, and gently press to get a nice coating. Repeat on opposite side. Set pepita-crusted sea bass fillets on a plate.

Heat ⅛ inch olive oil in a cast-iron pan or large sauté pan over medium heat. Place the sea bass fillets in the hot pan. Brown for about 2 minutes on each side, then transfer to a hot oven and bake until opaque throughout, about 5 minutes, more or less, depending how thick your fish is. Transfer to desired serving container. Serve with Kale Salad with Pineapple Jicama Salsa and Pepitas or over rice. Drizzle Coconut Chili Oil over fish and rice.

Crispy Tofu Tacos
with Ginger Sambal, Avocado, and Pickled Onion

SERVES 4

Ginger Sambal is a bright, bold sauce that is perfect for tofu. The crispy batter on the tofu adds another layer of crunch and flavor. Even if you're not a tofu fan, this is a really delicious taco. That said, there will always be people who don't like tofu no matter how good it is, so in that case, feel free to substitute the tofu for your favorite fish.

1 cup flour
1 teaspoon baking soda
1 tablespoon cornstarch
1¼ cups cold soda water
Vegetable oil, for frying
1 (10-ounce) package extra-firm organic tofu,
   cut into rectangular cubes
8 good-quality store-bought corn tortillas
1 avocado, sliced
Ginger Sambal Sauce (page 93)
Pickled Red Onion (recipe follows)
1 cup cilantro, chopped

Gently combine flour, baking soda, cornstarch, and club soda (take care not to overmix; a slightly lumpy batter is good). Fill a deep-walled, heavy pot one-third of the way with oil. Heat to 275°F.

Dry the tofu and then dip tofu rectangles in the batter. Gently fry tofu until golden brown. Place on a paper towel–lined tray until ready to assemble tacos.

To assemble, lay warm tortillas on platter, top with a piece of the crispy tofu, followed by avocado slices, a good spoonful of the Ginger Sambal, a small mound of pickled onion, and chopped cilantro.

Pickled Red Onion

Adding raw red beet pieces to the jar will make your pickled onion a lovely hot pink color. This awesome tip comes courtesy of my chef friend Christine Rivera. With some pickling liquid, this recipe should fill an eight-ounce mason jar.

1 cup white vinegar
1 tablespoon sugar
1 tablespoon salt

1 large red onion, sliced
½ small red beet, peeled and cut into a few pieces

Whisk first 3 ingredients together with ½ cup water. In a small saucepan, heat until mixture simmers and sugar has melted, then remove from heat. Place onion and beet pieces in a clean mason jar and pour in vinegar mixture. Let cool, cover. Store in the refrigerator. Pickled onions should last a few weeks. I think they taste best the first week; at my house they usually never make it past that.

Blackened Salmon
with Pineapple Jicama Salsa

❦ • ❧

SERVES 4

When blackening, getting a nice high heat on your pan is important. The trick is to oil the fish instead of the pan itself!

3 tablespoons chili powder
1 tablespoon dried cumin powder
1 tablespoon finely ground black pepper
1 teaspoon salt
4 (6-ounce) salmon fillets, pin bones removed
Vegetable oil
Pineapple Jicama Salsa (page 96)

Preheat oven to 375°F.

Toss first 4 ingredients together in a shallow bowl and set aside. Heat a large sauté pan (I strongly suggest using a cast-iron pan; lighter-weight-type pans just don't do as well for blackening) to high heat. Rub the salmon with oil and dredge flesh side in the blacken mix. Place the salmon in the pan and cook, undisturbed, around 1 minute per side. It will get smoky, so make sure you have good ventilation. Try to flip only once to get a nice blackened sear. Transfer to oven to cook the salmon through, around 5 minutes. Serve with Pineapple Jicama Salsa and your favorite rice.

Rack of Lamb
with Cumin, Cinnamon, and Cardamom Rub

This extremely aromatic rub does most of the work here. The smoky flavors of the rub meld beautifully with the bold, minty cilantro sauce. A rack of lamb is a pricey cut of meat, so be sure not to overcook the ribs.
I serve the ribs topped with a little touch of Minty Cilantro Dressing (page 100), giving them vibrancy both on the plate and in your mouth.

2 tablespoons cumin
2 tablespoons cinnamon
2 tablespoons cardamom
2 tablespoons coriander
¼ cup brown sugar
1 American rack of lamb (8 chops) or
    2 New Zealand racks (16 chops), chops
    separated into ribs
2 tablespoons olive oil
Minty Cilantro Dressing

Combine first five ingredients. Coat the lamb ribs with the dry rub, and then place the lamb in a large bowl or casserole, cover with plastic wrap, and refrigerate for at least 2 hours or overnight.

Coat a large cast-iron pan or skillet with oil. Warm over medium-high heat. Cook ribs in the pan to desired doneness, about 3 minutes per side. Add more oil as necessary. The desired effect is a nice seared coating of spices.

Transfer the cooked chops to a serving platter. To serve, drizzle with Minty Cilantro Dressing.

Grilled Chicken
with Chili Rub and Chipotle Sauce

❧ • ❧

SERVES 6

This is another recipe where I rely on the magic of a simple salt brine. I like to stick with what works—and this really does!

4 pounds chicken parts (legs, thighs, breasts, wings)
3 tablespoons salt
½ cup lime juice
4 chipotle chilies in adobo sauce
4 tablespoons brown sugar

1 cup olive oil
3 tablespoons chipotle chili powder (this may be spicy for some, feel free to substitute a mild chili powder)
2 tablespoons cumin

I always do a dry salt brine on bone-in chicken pieces when I roast chicken. It makes for a juicier, more flavorful bird, and it's so easy. Dry chicken with a paper towel. Rub the chicken all over with the salt, about ¾ tablespoon of salt per pound of chicken. Cover chicken loosely with plastic wrap and leave chicken in the fridge overnight or up to two nights.

Combine the lime juice, chilies, and brown sugar in a blender. With the blender running at low speed, add the olive oil through the top in a steady stream and continue to blend for about 4 minutes to form a nice emulsion. Set aside.

Toss chipotle chili powder and cumin together to make a rub. Sprinkle chipotle rub all over the chicken.

Prepare a charcoal fire or heat a gas grill to medium-high. Place chicken on grill skin-side down and cook until skin browns, about 8 minutes; turn over and cook another 8 minutes. If your chicken is grilling quickly and you're worried about it drying out, grill it to begin to get that nice, charred coating, then transfer it to an oven at 300°F until it's cooked through (chicken is considered cooked at an internal temperature of 165°F). This is the way I grill my chicken.

If you're committed to grilling only, pay attention to see if you have a slightly hotter side of the grill. If so, consider transferring smaller pieces (such as wings) to the cooler side of the grill partway through the process so they don't burn. As noted above, this is also great for the bigger pieces: once they have a nice char on all sides, move them over to the cooler side to cook all the way through and reduce the chances of drying out the meat.

Serve on large serving platter with Chipotle Lime Sauce (page 102).

Szechuan Peppercorn Scallops

It is no secret that Latinos love Asian food. Szechuan or Sichuan peppercorns (both spellings are common) are a good reason for that. If you haven't had them before, the flavor is unique but amazing. Because of the uniqueness of the flavor, I suggest starting off with a light sprinkling of the peppercorns, maybe even make a trial scallop so you can season the rest of the batch to your liking.

Olive oil, for greasing
1 pound sea scallops, side muscle removed
1-2 tablespoons ground roasted Szechuan
    peppercorns (recipe below)
Salt
2 tablespoons unsalted butter (¼ stick)
2 tablespoons soy sauce

Heat oil in a large sauté pan over medium-high heat. Season scallops with Szechuan peppercorns and light sprinkle of salt. Transfer seasoned scallops to heated pan (don't overcrowd the pan; do this in batches if necessary). Cook on one side until deep golden-brown color, about 3 minutes. Turn scallops, add butter and soy sauce to the pan, and add more olive oil if necessary. Finish cooking, about 3 minutes, until this side is golden brown, and spoon drippings on scallops. Serve as soon as possible. This goes great with rice and Avocado Salsa Cruda (page 99).

To Roast Szechuan Peppercorns

Pick through the peppercorns for any visible twigs or leaves. Place desired amount of peppercorns in a skillet on medium low. If peppercorns begin to smoke, lower the heat. Shake and stir peppercorns until they become fragrant and slightly darken. Do not burn them. When peppercorns have cooled, grind them in mini food processor or spice grinder. I like to store them in a clean mason jar. Stored properly, peppercorns should stay fresh for several months. As with ground pepper, Szechuan Peppercorns, once ground, will start to lose their flavor over time.

Grilled Marinated Pork with Potatoes and Serranos

SERVES 4–6

The first time I made this, I must say, I got a bit of resistance from my brother, Lee. He wanted to cook the pork tenderloin whole in the oven. In his defense, the oven is the way most people make pork tenderloin. I got my way, though, and we sliced it, marinated it, and on the grill it went. Even Lee now admits this is a good way to go!

1 pound pork tenderloin, sliced thin, about ¼-inch thick
Sweet Soy (page 109)
2 pounds boiled red potatoes, thinly sliced into half circles
Cilantro Lime Sauce (page 106)
1 large carrot, peeled and cut into matchsticks
½ cup green onion, chopped
½ pound fresh bean sprouts
2 red serrano chilies, sliced into thin circles
Peanuts, chopped (optional)

Let tenderloin marinate in Sweet Soy, about 2 hours.

Heat grill to high. Cook pork over indirect heat source until nice char marks appear (this should only take a few minutes), flip, and cook opposite side.

Gently toss potatoes with a generous coating of Cilantro Lime Sauce, and save any leftover sauce to serve on the side for anyone who would like more. Layer pork over potatoes. Separately toss carrot, green onion, bean sprouts, and serrano chilies together.

Top with carrot/bean sprout mixture, and sprinkle with chopped peanuts.

Chili Rellenos with Mango Salsa

At our restaurants, we have been serving these baked chili rellenos (without the batter) for years and guests love them. We serve them over rice with a big spoon of tomatillo sauce and mango salsa. The addition of grilled shrimp or baked carnitas is another good idea!

Mango Mint Salsa (page 98)
6 medium poblano chilies
1½ cups Monterey Jack cheese (more if you love cheese)
Tomatillo Sauce (page 98)

Blister chilies over stovetop flame on high heat, turning until blackened all over (alternatively, you can use a broiler). Place in a small bowl and cover tightly with plastic wrap. Let sit until chilies are soft, 15 to 20 minutes. Peel the skin and make a slit up the side of the chilies to remove seeds.

Preheat oven to 350°F. Stuff each chili with Jack cheese. Place chilies in cast-iron pan or low-sided ceramic dish. Heat rellenos until cheese is melted and bubbly, about 7 minutes.

Ladle with Tomatillo Sauce and dollop of Mango Salsa. This is fantastic over rice.

ABOUT ROASTING CHILIES

The first couple of times I roasted chilies for rellenos, I overroasted the chilies; they became too black and too limp. Getting the skin off was difficult and it made the chilies too flimsy to stuff with the cheese. This can also happen if the chilies aren't fresh enough. Start with a firm, fresh chili and blacken the chili in spots all over. Once you get the hang of this, the skin will come off easily as it rests in the plastic wrap–covered bowl.

Vegan Lomo

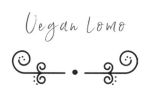

Lomo Saltado is a popular Peruvian dish typically made with strips of marinated steak stir-fried with tomatoes, onions, and potatoes (usually french-fried potatoes). This version is vegan, using tofu as its base. Rice accompanies Lomo, making it a two-starch dish.

Cilantro Lime Sauce (page 106)
4 large red potatoes
Kosher salt
Olive oil + more to grill onion and tofu
4 large Roma tomatoes, each cut into 6 wedges
1 tablespoon ground cumin
2 tablespoons ground chili powder
1 pound firm tofu, cut into thick strips
1 red onion, sliced

Preheat oven to 350°F.

Make Cilantro Lime Sauce, and refrigerate until ready to serve.

Cut the potatoes in half, put in large pot, and fill with water. Add a teaspoon of salt and bring to a boil. Cook the potatoes until they're tender but still holding their shape when pierced with a fork, about 30 minutes. Drain, and when cool enough to handle, cut each half into 3 wedges.

Coat two baking sheets with olive oil. Arrange the potato pieces on one, the tomatoes on the other. Drizzle each with olive oil, and season with a sprinkling of salt. Put both baking sheets in the oven. Roast the tomatoes for about 30 minutes, or until they are a deep red color. Remove from the oven and set aside. The potatoes will take a bit more time. Cook until crisp and brown, about 45 minutes.

Mix cumin and chili powder together. Gently toss tofu with the cumin/chili mix. Coat a large skillet with olive oil and warm over medium heat until hot but not smoking. Add the onion and cook about 4 minutes. Remove onion from pan and set aside. Add coated tofu to the pan. Stir and cook tofu until a slightly crisp coating forms, adding more olive oil if necessary. Add onion, roasted tomatoes, and potatoes to the pan and stir a bit to bring all the ingredients together. Serve the Lomo over steamed rice with a bowl of Cilantro Lime Sauce to be spooned out at the table.

Crispy Fish with Plantain Chips

SERVES 4

Fish and chips with a thick Latin accent, this meal brings fun to a classic. The plantains offer a healthy-ish alternative to traditional fries. And who needs tartar sauce? For an extra kick, serve with a side of Chipotle Cream!

2 cups regular flour
1 can lager beer
1½ cups soda water
1 tablespoon baking powder
1½ teaspoons cornstarch
1 teaspoon salt

3 green plantains
Oil, for frying
4 thick (6-ounce) cod or haddock fillets,
    cut in half
Chipotle Cream (page 100)

Whisk flour, beer, soda water, baking powder, cornstarch, and salt. Leave slightly lumpy, and refrigerate until ready to use.

Blot the plantain pieces dry with paper towels. Fill a large, heavy pot one-third of the way with oil. Heat to about 260°F or until small bubbles start to form. Gently add plantains to hot oil. They should sizzle but not spatter (throw one or two in first to test the temperature and adjust as needed). Cook about 4 minutes, until they're golden brown, turning the chips at least once to make sure all sides get crispy. Transfer the plantains to paper towel–lined plate to dry. Season them with salt, and set aside.

Remove any floating bits from the oil before starting to fry fish. Pat fish dry, coat fish in batter one at a time. Gently glide into oil. Fry, turning as necessary to get a nice golden-brown coating on all sides of the fish, about 4 to 6 minutes. Transfer to paper towel–lined baking sheet, blot dry, and sprinkle with salt. Serve hot with a side of Chipotle Cream.

To Peel Plantains

Cut both ends of the plantains off and then cut them in half. Make diagonal slits in the skins and then soak them in warm water for about 20 minutes. Peel the skins off and cut into ½-inch-thick chips. Soak them again in cold, salted water until ready to fry.

Best Shrimp Burrito

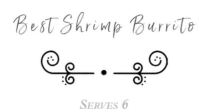

SERVES 6

Most everybody in my family loves to cook, but my son Ryan loves to EAT! This recipe is one of his favorites. I've never been much of a burrito person, but this one is an exception.

Black Beans (page 50)
Basic Salsa Recipe (page 93)
Chipotle Cream (page 100)
3 cups Jack cheese, shredded
3 cups cabbage, shredded
Olive oil
3-4 jalapeños, thinly sliced
1 pound shrimp, shelled and deveined, tails off
Salt
6 extra-large fluffy flour tortillas

Warm black beans in saucepan and have ready to go along with Basic Salsa, Chipotle Cream, cheese, and cabbage.

Heat a large, heavy-duty sauté pan over medium high and coat with olive oil. Place jalapeños first and let cook in pan about 2 minutes. Add 2 cups of the Basic Salsa to pan and cook about 2 minutes, just enough to start to warm the salsa. Add shrimp to pan and cook until shrimp begins to turn pink and is cooked through. Add salt to taste. Turn off heat.

Grill tortillas and assemble burritos. Layer ingredients in warm tortilla as follows: drained ladle of black beans topped with Jack cheese followed by warm shrimp/jalapeño/salsa mixture. Spread with Chipotle Cream and top with cabbage. Roll burrito.

Turkey Picadillo

SERVES 4–6

It seems like every Latin country has its own version of a Picadillo. Cuba, Spain, Puerto Rico, and Mexico each have their own twist, but the one common factor in all of them is that the main ingredient is some kind of ground meat.

Picadillo was a staple in our house while I was growing up. My mom liked to make it because it is a relatively fast dinner to throw together. For us kids, it was our favorite comfort food. My version is a little different from my mom's because I make it with ground white turkey, while her version is a bit more traditional with ground beef.

Olive oil
1 yellow onion, finely chopped (about 1 cup)
3 cloves garlic, minced
1 teaspoon ground cumin
1½ pounds ground turkey meat
2 medium red potatoes, ¼-inch dice
½ cup green olives with pimentos, cut in half
3 tablespoons capers
⅓ cup raisins
Salt

Heat 2 tablespoons of olive oil in a large sauté pan over medium heat. Add the onion and garlic and cook until soft and translucent, about 3 minutes. Add the cumin, stir to combine, then add the turkey meat. Use a fork to break up the meat, and cook until the turkey is no longer pink, about 5 to 7 minutes. Add potatoes, olives, capers, and raisins. Lower heat and simmer until potatoes are cooked through, about 10 minutes. Salt to taste. Serve over short-grain brown rice.

Three Piggies Tacos

Bacon, carnitas, and chicharrones—the only thing that could make this combination better would be to put it all in a taco, right? Ah ha, here it is! The Three Piggies Taco goes great with a Blackberry Chili Margarita.

1½ teaspoons ground cumin
1½ teaspoons dried oregano
1½ teaspoons ground chili powder
Salt
2 pounds boneless pork shoulder, fat trimmed
1 can lager beer
1½ cups shredded Jack cheese

½ pound bacon, cooked crispy then chopped
Corn tortillas, good-quality store-bought or homemade
Isabel Sauce (page 107)
1 (5-ounce) bag store-bought chicharrones
1 cup cilantro, chopped

Preheat oven to 300°F.

Combine the cumin, oregano, chili powder, and salt in a small bowl to make a seasoning mix. Cut pork into 4 pieces. Rub the seasoning on the pieces of pork, and place the pork in a Pyrex casserole dish or other ovenproof baking vessel. Pour beer into baking vessel. Cover pork tightly with aluminum foil. Bake in the preheated oven. Check after 1 hour for tenderness (take care when opening foil, the steam will be hot). The desired result is meat that is fork-tender. Baking time to achieve this tender meat is about 90 minutes.

Remove the foil, raise to 375°F, and bake until the carnitas is nicely browned, about 10 minutes. While carnitas is baking, prepare the remaining ingredients. When meat has cooled enough to handle, shred carnitas into desired-size pieces.

When cooking corn tortillas, add shredded Jack cheese to the cooked side of the tortilla after flipping once. This will give you a gooey, melted cheese layer. Add the chopped bacon on top of the melted cheese followed by the shredded carnitas. Remove from oven and proceed layering with Isabel Sauce, chicharrones, and cilantro.

Grilled Ribeye Steak with Heirloom Tomato, Avocado, and Cotija Salad

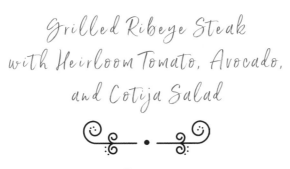

SERVES 4

This recipe's quick and simple marinade will give my favorite cut of meat—ribeye—a nice char. Pairing it with the recommended salad lightens up the heaviness of the steak.

1½ -2 pounds boneless ribeye steak
¼ cup Sweet Soy (page 109)
Finishing salt, for steak
Cilantro Lime Sauce (page 106)
Heirloom Tomato, Avocado, and Cotija Salad with Roasted Tomato Vinaigrette (page 33)

Drizzle the steak with the Sweet Soy and let marinate in clean (preferably) glass container for about 2 hours. Let excess marinade drip off steaks and let steaks come to room temperature. Heat charcoal grill or indoor grill over burner on high heat. Grill steak about 6 minutes each side or until deep grill marks are achieved. Let steaks rest about 8 minutes before slicing. Sprinkle with finishing salt, if desired, but take care as the soy marinade is salty. Drizzle with Cilantro Lime Sauce and serve with Heirloom Tomato, Avocado, and Cotija Salad with Roasted Tomato Vinaigrette.

Chicken Lettuce Wraps

SERVES 4

Lettuce wraps are my go-to meal when my jeans are feeling just a little too tight. It works, believe me, and it doesn't feel like you're eating diet food because it's not diet food—it's just real good food.

Olive oil
3 (8-ounce) boneless skinless chicken breast
    halves, cut into strips
Salt
8 nice and sturdy large leaves (romaine, green
    leaf, or butter lettuce)
Any combination or all of the ingredients listed below:
    ¼ medium red onion, thinly sliced
    1 cucumber, cut into thick matchsticks
    4 medium radishes, thinly sliced
    Small bunch of fresh cilantro, mint, basil (any combination)
    1 avocado, sliced
    1 red jalapeño, sliced
Cilantro Lime Sauce (page 106)

Coat a large sauté pan with olive oil and heat pan over medium high. Put the chicken in the pan and cook, stirring, until the chicken is lightly browned and cooked through, about 7 minutes. Sprinkle with desired salt.

To serve, have guests top each lettuce leaf with chicken, desired accompaniments, and Cilantro Lime Sauce.

Ropa Vieja

A classic of Cuban cuisine, Ropa Vieja means "old clothes," and the shreds of meat are meant to look like just that. Not the savoriest image, I know—but the dish itself is well-loved, delicious, and long-standing. Every family has its own way of making this recipe their own. This is mine.
Serve this with steamed white rice and sliced green olives.
If you have any leftovers it makes a great breakfast. Scramble eggs into the meat mixture and serve it with some warm tortillas.

BEEF & BROTH

1 flank steak, about 1½ pounds, cut across the grain into 4 pieces
1 yellow onion, halved
4 cloves garlic, smashed and peeled
2 bay leaves
½ teaspoon ground cumin

VEGETABLES

3 tablespoons olive oil
½ medium yellow onion, sliced
2 cloves garlic, peeled and minced
1 red bell pepper, seeds discarded and thinly sliced
¾ cup white wine
2 tablespoons tomato paste
Reserved broth from the meat
½ teaspoon salt
1 chipotle chili in adobo sauce, minced
½ cup green onion, sliced

Combine the steak, onion, garlic, bay leaves, and cumin in a large pot and add enough water to cover completely. Bring to a boil and then reduce to a gentle simmer. Cook until meat is very tender and falling apart, about 2 to 2½ hours.

Remove the meat from the liquid, reserving the broth but discarding the solids. Place in a bowl to cool. When cool enough to handle, shred the meat.

Heat the olive oil over a medium-high flame until hot but not smoking. Add the onion, garlic, and red bell pepper. Sauté until the vegetables are tender and translucent, about 4 minutes. Add the white wine and tomato paste. Stir well and cook for about 5 minutes, stirring frequently and lowering the flame if necessary. Add the reserved beef broth, salt, and chipotle chili. Cook the mixture at a strong simmer for about 5 minutes so that the liquid thickens. Add the beef and stir. Cook until the beef is heated through, then top with the green onion.

Quinoa with Green Olives and Red Onion

Quinoa is a grain as ancient as the Incas themselves, who held this crop to be sacred. For more than six thousand years, it has been an important complete food, called "the mother of all grains" for its super-high protein content. Here it serves as the perfect backdrop for the bold flavors of olive and red onion.

1 cup quinoa
½ teaspoon salt
¼ cup olive oil
½ red onion, diced
½ cup red bell pepper, diced
¾ cup green olives, pitted and halved
3 tablespoons lemon juice
1 teaspoon ground cumin
½ cup cilantro, chopped

Place the quinoa and salt in a medium saucepan and cover with 2 cups of water. Bring to a boil, and then reduce to a simmer. Cover and cook until the water has been absorbed and the quinoa is tender, 10 to 15 minutes. Set aside.

Heat 2 tablespoons of the olive oil over medium heat. Add the onion and sauté until soft and translucent, then add the diced red bell pepper. Continue cooking until the red bell pepper has softened, about 3 minutes. Add the olives, stirring well to combine, and cook for 1 more minute. Transfer the sautéed vegetables to a medium bowl.

Add the quinoa, lemon juice, the remaining 2 tablespoons of olive oil, cumin, and chopped cilantro. Toss well to combine.

Serve the quinoa warm, at room temperature, or cold.

Sauces & Salsas

And a Few Other Fierce-Flavored Condiments

I would have to say my strongest cooking asset is my ability to make a simple sauce that is really good. This is what can turn a meal on the border of boring into something special. Use this chapter, and get creative with it! As you've seen, I use many of these recipes several times throughout the book, and I would go as far as saying you could put Cilantro Lime Sauce on just about any of the recipes in the book and it would make every one of them taste better.

I'm also a fan of layering sauces—any of these sauces go great with each other. I really like the two sauce/salsa way of eating. For example, Cilantro Lime works wonderfully with Isabel Sauce as well as Avocado Salsa Cruda or Mango Mint Salsa or Chipotle Corn Salsa, and I can go on and on. So try these recipes and don't be afraid to multi-sauce!

Basic Salsa

Salsa is not just for tortilla chips and tacos. You can use it as a pick-me-up to a soup base, to throw on a chicken while roasting, or as a base sauce for grilled shrimp (Best Shrimp Burrito page 80).

1 (28-ounce) can plum tomatoes and
   their juices
4 yellow chilies (or 2 jalapeños)
2 cloves garlic, crushed and peeled

1 cup cilantro, tough stem ends removed
½ yellow onion, peeled and roughly
   chopped
Salt

Combine all the ingredients in the work bowl of a food processor and pulse until the mixture is well combined but still chunky.

Store the salsa covered in the refrigerated for up to 3 days.

Ginger Sambal

MAKES 1 CUP

This sauce is bold and bright in a big way, and it turns out a beautiful color. I tend to use it mostly with vegetarian/vegan dishes, but it works well with fish or shrimp also.

¼ cup sambal olick chili paste
¼ cup fresh ginger, chopped and peeled
¼ cup rice wine vinegar
2 tablespoons white sugar
2 tablespoons dark sesame oil

Purée all ingredients. This sambal keeps refrigerated for up to 3 days.

Pineapple Jicama Salsa (page 96)

*Mango Mint Salsa
(page 98)*

Chipotle Corn Salsa

When using fresh summer corn, I just slice it off the cob, no cooking or blanching. If you have good, fresh corn, it will already be sweet and crunchy. If you can't get your hands on fresh corn, use a good-quality frozen corn (it works much better then canned). If you do use frozen corn, make sure to thaw it first in a separate container by putting the corn in a small strainer over a bowl, for example, to let it thaw. You don't want the water from the frozen corn to dilute the chipotle/juice mixture that makes this salsa so good.

2 chipotle chilies in adobo, minced
½ cup orange juice
2 tablespoons brown sugar
2 cups roasted corn kernels (about 3 ears of fresh corn)
½ red onion, diced

1 red bell pepper, seeds removed, small dice
½ cup cilantro leaves, rinsed and roughly chopped
Salt

Whisk first three ingredients in a bowl and set aside. Toss remaining ingredients together in another bowl, and combine with chipotle/lime/brown sugar mixture. Season with salt to taste. This salsa keeps refrigerated for up to 2 days.

Olive and Caper Salsa Cruda

This salsa is especially good on fish but it also can perk up chicken breasts. To layer flavors, try this salsa with the Chimmicurri Sauce on page 101.

¼ cup red onion, small dice
¼ cup pitted green olives, sliced
¼ cup pitted kalamata olives, sliced
1 avocado, diced

2 tablespoons capers
¼ cup olive oil
Salt

Toss the first five ingredients together and drizzle with olive oil. Set aside in refrigerator until ready to serve. Salt to taste but be careful—olives and capers are salty. Best used the day made.

Pineapple Jicama Salsa

Using fresh pineapple is best for this, but in a pinch, canned or frozen works quite well.

1½ cups pineapple, diced
1 cup jicama, diced
¼ cup red onion, diced
1 red jalapeño, seeded, minced

2 teaspoons brown sugar
¼ cup cilantro, chopped
¼ cup fresh mint, chopped
Salt (optional)

Combine first 5 ingredients in a bowl, then gently stir in cilantro and mint. Season salsa with salt to taste. This salsa keeps refrigerated for up to 2 days.

Orange Chili Oil

My all-time favorite cookbook is Barbara Tropp's China Moon Cookbook. *I became so enamored with the book that I had to go to the Cafe in San Francisco. I took a plane by myself (I was just a teen) for the day just to go to lunch there (my parents had no idea). I was blown away. The food was nothing like I had ever experienced before. It was my first and one of my best foodie adventures.*

This Chili Oil is inspired by my love of Barbara Tropp's famous Orange Chili Oil. RIP Barbara, I wish I could have met you! It's been more than thirty years since my trek to China Moon Cafe and it still inspires me to this day. I use this chili oil in one form or another like crazy! The customers at my restaurants are used to seeing it as a side on some of my most popular dishes, and you'll see it in recipes throughout this book. Get ready to get hooked!

Zest from 3 large oranges, washed
   thoroughly before zesting
½ cup dried red chile flakes
1 large garlic clove, peeled and lightly
   smashed

1 cup vegetable oil (a good-quality corn
   or peanut oil works well)
½ cup sesame oil

Combine ingredients in a heavy, nonaluminum saucepan on medium-low heat. The goal is to heat the oil and ingredients slow and low and for the mixture to slightly bubble (if the bubbles get big, turn it off—you don't want to burn the ingredients) for about 10 minutes. Adjust the heat accordingly. Remove from the heat and let stand until cool or overnight.

Transfer the oil and seasonings into a clean glass mason jar. Discard the garlic. If refrigerated, chili oil can last a couple months.

I suggest using organic oranges. If you don't have a good zester, you can peel away the orange skin with a good peeler (try and leave as much of the white pith behind as possible) and finely mince.

Orange Chili Oil Dressing

MAKES ABOUT 1 ¼ CUPS

¾ cup orange chili oil (make sure there is plenty of the chili flakes and orange rind)
¼ cup soy sauce (more or less depending on personal taste)

Stir above two ingredients together. If refrigerated, chili oil dressing can last a couple of months.

Coconut Chili Oil

MAKES ABOUT 1 CUP

This is another fantastic variation. Try it on grilled fish with rice to soak up all of the chili-coconut goodness.

¼ cup orange chili oil (stirred well so you get a good amount of the orange rind and chili flakes)
2 tablespoons soy sauce
2 tablespoons rice wine vinegar
2 tablespoons brown sugar
½ can full-fat coconut milk

Whisk chili oil, soy sauce, rice wine vinegar, and brown sugar until combined. Slowly stir in the coconut milk. If properly refrigerated, this sauce can last 3 days.

Tomatillo Sauce

Small green tomatoes with a papery husk that is easily peeled away, tomatillos have a fruity and zesty flavor that makes them an appealing alternative to red salsas. As an ancient Mexican ingredient, tomatillos are a culinary cornerstone of Latin cooking. As a modern American salsa, this is a deliciously low-fat way to boost flavor.

½ pound of tomatillos, husks
   removed, rinsed
1 jalapeño, seeds discarded

1 clove of garlic, peeled
Salt

Preheat the oven to 350°F.

Place the tomatillos, jalapeño, and garlic on a baking sheet. Transfer to the preheated oven and slow roast until the tomatillos begin to crack, about 20 minutes.

Slide the baking tray into a broiler set on high for 2–3 minutes to slightly blacken the tomatillos. Transfer the contents of the baking tray (including any juice from the tomatillos) into the work bowl of a food processor and puree. Season to taste with salt. This salsa keeps refrigerated for up to 3 days.

Mango Mint Salsa

Exotic, flavorful, but oh-so-easy to make, this mix of fruit and mint adds color and a fresh flavor kick to meats, fish, and, of course, chips. For this salsa, look for fruit that is newly ripe—flavorful, but still firm enough to hold its own.

1 mango, medium dice
1 jalapeños, seeds discarded, minced
¼ cup red onion, diced

¼ cup mint leaves, chopped
2 tablespoons cilantro, roughly chopped
   (optional)

Combine all the ingredients in a mixing bowl and toss gently to combine. This salsa keeps refrigerated for up to 2 days.

Avocado Salsa Cruda

MAKES 2 CUPS

Nice and simple, but make sure to enjoy the beautiful bounty of tomatoes during their season. Use any combination of your favorite variety.

2 tablespoons olive oil
1 tablespoon lime juice
1 cup cherry tomatoes, cut into halves and
    quarters depending on size
¼ small red onion

½ cup cilantro, chopped, tough stems
    roughly chopped
½ avocado, diced
Salt

Whisk the olive oil with lime juice. Gently combine with the tomatoes, onion, cilantro, and avocado. Salt to taste. Serve immediately, best used the day made.

Roasted Tomato Vinaigrette

This intensely flavored dressing gives any salad instant Latin flair. If there's a loaf of good bread nearby, I can't stop myself from dipping.

MAKES 1½ CUPS

2 Roma tomatoes, cut into quarters
1 red jalapeño or red serrano chili
1 garlic clove
½ cup extra-virgin olive oil + more to
    drizzle on tomatoes to roast

Salt
3 tablespoons rice wine vinegar
1 teaspoon brown sugar

Preheat oven to 300°F.

Place tomatoes, chili, and garlic clove on a baking tray, drizzle lightly with olive oil, and season with a light sprinkle of salt. Slow roast in oven until the tomatoes and chilies appear shrunken and have started to caramelize, about 25 minutes. Set aside to cool.

Transfer all ingredients to blender, pour a steady stream of the olive oil while puréeing, and salt to taste. This dressing keeps refrigerated for up to 2 days.

Chipotle Mayo

As you have probably noticed, I use chipotle chilies all over this book; they are so smoky and flavorful that they transform something as simple as mayo into a delicious sauce. They are dried, smoked jalape-ños sold in a spicy tomato sauce called adobo. This Chipotle Mayo is one of my favorite things to serve with seafood.

3 chipotle chilies in adobo (use more or less depending on your tolerance for heat)
1 cup mayonnaise

Place the chipotle chilies in a blender or food processor. Purée until smooth. Pour the purée into a small mixing bowl along with the mayo. Whisk well to combine.

The Chipotle Mayo keeps refrigerated for up to 3 days.

VARIATION
To make Chipotle Cream, substitute your favorite thick sour cream for mayonnaise.

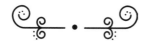

Minty Cilantro Dressing

This fragrant mix of herbs can be used as a condiment for fish, meat, poultry, or veggies, a fruit salad, and of course with the rack of lamb.

½ cup cilantro leaves
½ cup mint leaves
¼ cup olive oil

3 tablespoons lemon juice
1 teaspoon honey

Combine the ingredients in a blender or food processor. Pulse until combined. Best used the day made.

Chimichurri Sauce

Bold, bold, bold—that's what this sauce is! It will turn up the flavor on anything you are making.

¼ cup cilantro, roughly chopped

3 tablespoons lime juice

2 teaspoons fresh oregano (if using dried, 1 teaspoon)

3 garlic cloves, roughly chopped

2 teaspoons chili flakes

½ cup olive oil

Salt

Combine first six ingredients in a blender or food processor and pulse until combined, but still has some texture. Salt to taste. Best used the day made.

Avocado Sauce (a.k.a. Omar Sauce)

MAKES 1¼ CUPS

Omar is a talented chef that has worked for me for many years. He created this sauce and it is a much-loved staple in the restaurants. Drizzle it on tacos, tostadas, even eggs. If you like avocado, you've found your sauce!

½ ripe avocado, peeled and pitted

½ cup cilantro, chopped

1 large jalapeño, roughly chopped

1 garlic clove

½ cup soy or hemp milk (more or less to desired consistency)

Salt

Place first four ingredients into heavy-duty blender. Pour a steady stream of the hemp milk while puréeing ingredients together to form a smooth, fluffy sauce. Salt to taste. Best used the day made.

Guajilo Sauce

I love Guajilo Sauce, and not because it's so great on its own. Guajilo Sauce is a base to make other sauces, the most basic being enchilada sauce. It adds an earthiness to everything you use it in. In this book, I added it to a simple tomato soup, transforming it from basic to a special dish. If you have leftover sauce, try it in your Bloody Maria recipe.

8 dried guajillo chilies, cleaned, stemmed, seeded
1 garlic clove
Sea salt

In a medium saucepan, boil 5 cups of water and turn off heat. Submerge chilies—you will need to push them down occasionally to keep them underwater. Soak chilies until they become very tender, about 30 minutes. Transfer chilies to blender, reserve cooking liquid, and add garlic clove. Purée while adding 1 cup reserved water, adding more water as needed to achieve a smooth sauce. Add salt to taste. Guajilo sauce will keep for a week if refrigerated properly.

Chipotle Lime Sauce

This sauce complements any meat straight off the barbecue, especially chicken. It's tangy and a little sweet with just the right amount of heat.

½ cup lime juice
3 chipotle chilies in adobo sauce
3 tablespoons brown sugar
1 cup olive oil
Salt

Combine lime juice, chilies, and brown sugar in blender. With blender running, pour olive oil in a steady stream to combine. Add salt to taste. This sauce keeps refrigerated for up to 5 days.

Hibiscus Syrup

There are so many things to be made with this amazing syrup—it works for cocktails with tequila and rum, or for the more adventurous, mezcal. It also makes a great iced tea—just add water, ice, and a few mint sprigs. Or you can use it as a drizzle over vanilla ice cream or as it is used with the Mango, Jicama, and Watermelon Salad on page 41.

2 cups sugar
1 cup dried hibiscus flowers

Combine 2 cups of water with the sugar and hibiscus flowers in a medium saucepan. Bring to a boil, then reduce heat to a simmer until sugar is completely dissolved, flowers soften, and mixture has a slight syrup consistency. In a fine-mesh strainer, press solids with a wooden spoon. Discard solids, let syrup cool. Store in a clean, preferably glass container.

Cotija Ranch Dressing

MAKES 2 CUPS

This is a variation on a simple ranch dressing. The addition of the cotija cheese goes great with the creamy twang of the original dressing.

1 clove garlic, minced
⅛ teaspoon salt
¼ cup lime juice

1 cup sour cream
½ cup cotija cheese, crumbled
About ¼ cup half-and-half or buttermilk

Mash garlic with a spoon and then sprinkle with about ⅛ teaspoon salt. Mash some more then add lime juice and give it a quick stir. Add sour cream and cotija cheese and mix to combine. Add half-and-half or buttermilk, adding more or less or none to achieve desired creaminess. I like this dressing on the thick side but still pourable. Refrigerate until ready to use. Best used within 2 days.

Orange-Oregano Dressing

Layers of flavors make this a particularly delicious salad dressing. Don't stop at the salad—this dressing makes an excellent drizzle on steamed greens, roasted vegetables, or even grilled fish.

¼ cup orange juice
¼ cup red wine vinegar
1 teaspoon dried oregano
1 teaspoon red chili flakes
1 tablespoon brown sugar
⅔ cup olive oil

Combine everything but the olive oil in a small bowl. Drizzle the olive oil in a slow stream while whisking the ingredients together. This dressing keeps refrigerated for up to 2 days.

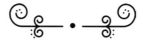

Tequila Honey Dressing

MAKES ¾ CUP

I really enjoy this dressing with citrus, which is why I recommend it with the Citrus Salad with Arugula (page 38).

¼ cup honey
¼ cup gold tequila
2 tablespoons olive oil

Combine the honey and tequila and whisk until thoroughly blended. Add the olive oil and whisk again before serving. This dressing will last several weeks refrigerated.

Heirloom Tomato Pico de Gallo

Heirloom tomatoes make such pretty salsa. I try to use them as much as I can when they are in season. When heirlooms are out of season, feel free to substitute your tomato of choice.

2-3 heirloom tomatoes, cut into medium dice, or 1 pint heirloom cherry tomatoes, cut in halves or quarters depending on size
1-2 jalapeños, finely chopped

¼ red onion, thinly sliced
½ cup cilantro, chopped
1 tablespoon olive oil
Juice of 1 lime
Salt

Gently toss first four ingredients together. Whisk olive oil and the juice of the lime and pour over salsa cruda. Sprinkle with salt to taste. Pico de Gallo is best used the day made.

Cumin Vinaigrette

MAKES 1 CUP

Cumin Vinaigrette is one of my favorite dressings because it has so much flavor. Many times, I'll layer it with another sauce or dressing to add some depth into a simple dish. For example, it goes great with the Cotija Ranch Dressing on the Mexican Ensalada Buena (page 34). This pair brings you the tart, bright Cumin Vin and the creamy Cotija Ranch.

⅓ cup rice wine vinegar
1 teaspoon brown sugar
1 teaspoon ground cumin
⅔ cup olive oil

Whisk all ingredients together until combined. This dressing will last several weeks refrigerated. When ready to serve, bring to room temperature and give it another quick whisk.

Cilantro Vinaigrette

This is quick to make and useful beyond salads. You can drizzle it on just about everything, from grilled vegetables to grilled meats, to add flavor and flair.

¼ cup red wine vinegar
1 clove garlic, peeled and minced
⅔ cup cilantro, rinsed and roughly chopped
½ cup olive oil
Salt

Combine first three ingredients in a blender or food processor. While processing, pour a steady stream of olive oil. Salt to taste. This vinaigrette keeps refrigerated for up to 2 days.

Cilantro Lime Sauce

MAKES ABOUT 1 CUP

As a chef, it's hard to pick favorite recipes, but this sauce is way up there. This is the sauce I promised you can be used on everything from grilled corn to steak. Really, you could put it on just about anything and it will make whatever it is taste better. Besides the distinctive flavors of cilantro and lime, the sauce adds a nice color to the plate.

¾ cup chopped cilantro
¼ cup lime juice
½ cup olive oil
Salt

Combine cilantro and lime juice in blender or small food processor. Purée on low while pouring in the olive oil in a steady stream. Blend until combined. Add salt to taste. Best used the day made.

Sometimes cilantro will give a slightly bitter taste. If this is happening, just add a bit of honey, and the honey will fix it.

Isabel Sauce

I always have this sauce ready to go in large batches at my house. We use it like ketchup—on every-thing! Bold and tart, this one pairs well with Cilantro Lime Sauce. On its own, it can jump-start just about any taco, egg dish, or fish meat—it is a perfectly spicy-sweet hot sauce. The Roma tomatoes add freshness and can also curb the heat. Use more or less depending on how spicy you like your hot sauce. If you like it really spicy, omit the tomatoes altogether. Feel free to make half a batch to start, but if your home is anything like mine, you'll be up to a full batch in no time.

½ cup chipotle chilies with adobo sauce, roughly chopped

½ cup red jalapeños or fresno chilies, stemmed, chopped

¼ cup yellow onion, chopped

2 garlic cloves, chopped

½ cup + 2 tablespoons white vinegar

¼ cup white sugar

2 Roma tomatoes, chopped

Salt

Purée first seven ingredients together. Salt to taste. This sauce keeps refrigerated for up to 3 days.

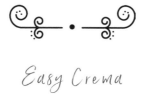

Easy Crema

1 clove garlic, minced

½ teaspoon salt

3 tablespoons lime juice

1 cup thick sour cream

Mash garlic with a spoon, then sprinkle with about ½ teaspoon salt. Mash some more, add lime juice, and give it a quick stir. Add sour cream and mix to combine. Easy Crema keeps refrigerated for up to 2 days.

SAUCES & SALSAS   107

Jalapeño Honey Butter

Jalapeño Honey Butter

MAKES ABOUT ¼ CUP

This butter is the best! Even if you just spread it on some crusty grilled bread, it is splendid.

1 stick butter, slightly softened

1 jalapeño, roasted, stemmed, seeded,
   chopped

2 tablespoons honey

Combine ingredients in the bowl of a small food processor or blender until just combined. Don't overprocess; it's nice when the jalapeño still has some texture. This can also be done by hand in a bowl. The butter keeps refrigerated for up to 3 days.

* * *

Sweet Soy

I use this thick, syrupy reduction as a marinade. Not only is it simple to make, but it has a long shelf life, making it a great flavoring to keep on hand.

MAKES 1½ CUPS

1 cup soy sauce

1 cup sugar

Combine soy sauce and sugar in a small saucepan. Bring to a low boil over medium heat, and reduce heat to low. Simmer until the sugar has melted and sauce has slightly thickened, about 15 minutes. Remove from heat and let cool completely. Store in a clean, preferably glass, jar with a tight lid in the refrigerator. Sweet Soy will last a few months if refrigerated properly. Bring to room temperature before using as this will thicken when cold.

* * *

Chili Cumin Rub

I use this simple rub to flavor many things, including beans, rice, chicken, and pork—this list can go on and on. It not only has great flavor, but it can give anything you use it for good color!

¼ cup mild ground chili powder

2 tablespoons ground cumin

Toss chili powder and cumin together. Store in an airtight container. It should last a couple of months while retaining its flavor.

Red Bell Pepper Sofrito

MAKES 1½ CUPS

Sofrito is a simple paste Latin cooks from Cuba, Dominican Republic, Mexico, Puerto Rico, and Spain make to use as a base for a multitude of recipes. My version is pretty straightforward; there are probably thousands of versions throughout Latin America. My mom makes a batch every few days and stores it in a mason jar in the fridge. She scoops it out to season soups, beans, chicken, shrimp, etc. It will bump up the flavor in anything you add it to, guaranteed!

½ cup olive oil
1 red bell pepper, seeded and deveined, diced
½ large yellow onion, medium dice
4 cloves garlic, peeled and chopped

Heat the olive oil in a medium straight-sided sauté pan over medium heat. Add the pepper, onion, and garlic and sauté until soft and the onion is starting to caramelize. Take care not to burn the garlic; you want it golden brown but you don't want any bitter or burned garlic taste. Let cool down a bit. Purée. Sofrito will keep refrigerated for up to 2 days.

Sofrito Vinaigrette

MAKES ABOUT 1¾ CUPS

½ cup Red Bell Pepper Sofrito (page 110)
¾ cup extra-virgin olive oil
¼ cup balsamic vinegar

2 teaspoons brown sugar
2 teaspoons rosemary, minced

Whisk all ingredients together until well blended. This vinaigrette will keep refrigerated for up to 2 days. Bring to room temperature and whisk before using.

Raspberry Purée

A few years ago when I was serving dessert with a raspberry purée to a cooking class, I noticed a few of the attendees starting to cough. First it was a little bit, but then pretty soon the whole class was coughing. One of my cooks had accidentally labeled chili purée as raspberry purée! I thought I was going to have a heart attack. When the coughing fits subsided and I was composed, we all had a good laugh—and, as it turned out, the chili actually tasted good with the chocolate cake I had served it with!

Raspberry purée is a wonderful ingredient with many uses. At my restaurants, we use it to accompany our pancakes, French toast, and desserts. It is a versatile sauce because it goes well with so many flavors from chocolate to coconut and beyond. I also offer a variation below for raspberry compote. Use this for a chunkier, jammier consistency.

1 (16-ounce bag) frozen raspberries
½ cup sugar

Combine the raspberries and the sugar in a medium saucepan. Warm over medium heat and, stirring occasionally, simmer until the berries have broken down, about 10 minutes.

Transfer the mixture to a food processor and purée. Pass through a strainer to remove seeds. Store purée in refrigerator until ready to serve.

Raspberry Compote

MAKES 3 CUPS

I use compote when layering, like with the Coconut and Raspberry Chia Breakfast Pudding (page 147), or to spoon over something like rice pudding.

1 (16-ounce) bag frozen raspberries
¼ cup honey

Combine raspberries and honey in a medium saucepan. Warm over medium heat until slightly thickened and raspberries have a jammy consistency. Let cool. Store in the refrigerator until ready to serve.

Drinks

Latin food has always been synonymous with cool drinks—and cooler cocktails. Even cool coffee. Why does coffee taste so good in all the Latin countries I've been to? Maybe it's because they love it so much. For that matter, most beverages taste better with the Latin touch. What would we do without margaritas, mojitos, piña coladas, etc.?

Blackberry Chili Margarita (a.k.a. Super Linda)

At the restaurant, we named this cocktail Super Linda, which means "super pretty." It is also super buena, which means "super good"!

½ ounce lime juice
½ ounce simple syrup (or agave nectar)
1 ounce blackberry purée, recipe follows
2 ounces arbol chili-infused tequila, recipe follows

Place all ingredients with ice in a cocktail tin. Shake vigorously. Pour over ice with or without a salt-rimmed glass.

Blackberry Puree

1 (16-ounce) package frozen blackberries
¼ cup + ½ tablespoons sugar

Combine the blackberries and sugar in a medium saucepan. Bring to a simmer and let cook until blackberries are completely thawed and have taken on a jammy consistency, about 10 minutes.
Transfer mixture to a food processor or blender and puree. Pass through a strainer to remove the seeds. Hold puree in refrigerator until ready to serve.
Transfer

Arbol Chili-Infused Tequila

1 bottle blanco tequila 100% agave
½ cup dried chilies de arbol, cleaned, stemmed, and cracked up a bit so the seeds are somewhat exposed

Combine tequila and chilies in a large mason jar or other large glass vessel and tighten the lid. (If you don't have a large glass vessel, any large clean container with a lid will work.) Let chilies and tequila infuse overnight. I always do a taste test after a few hours to get a read on how hot the chilies are (chilies can vary in spiciness). If you want a spicier tequila, let it infuse longer. If your tequila gets too spicy for you, you can always add more tequila to mellow out the flavor. When tequila has achieved your desired spice level, strain out all solids. Return tequila to bottle and label *muy caliente*!

Lemon and Green Tea Sangria

Lemon and Green Tea Sangria

White sangria isn't seen as frequently as red, which might be why I like it so much. As a summer party drink, this is light and refreshing.

3 bags green tea
2/3 cup honey, more or less as desired
1 cup lemon juice
1 bottle white wine
2 lemons, thinly sliced, seeded for garnish

Bring 2½ cups of water to boil. Take off heat, add tea bags, and let steep about 5 minutes. Remove tea bags, add honey, and stir to dissolve. Allow to cool. In a large pitcher, pour tea, stir in lemon juice, and then add the wine. Chill in the refrigerator for at least 1 hour. Serve over ice and garnish with lemon wheels.

Mango Iced Tea

MAKES 8 CUPS

A delicious, fruity way to lighten up black tea. Feel free to add more mango if desired.

5 black tea bags
2 cups frozen mango purée or mango nectar
Sugar (optional, I prefer mine without added sugar)
Mango slices, for garnish (optional)

Boil 7 cups of water, remove from heat, add tea bags, and let steep 5 minutes. Remove tea bags and add frozen mango purée or mango nectar. If using frozen mango purée, stir until dissolved. If using nectar, stir until combined. Add sugar to taste, if desired. Serve over ice in tall glasses and garnish with mango slices, if desired.

Tequila Mule

Refreshing, light, and just a little bit spicy.

1 cup white tequila 100% agave
3 jalapeños, cut into rounds
¼ cup Cointreau

½ cup lime juice
1 bottle good-quality ginger beer
Lime wedges, for garnish

Add tequila and jalapeño wheels to a sturdy pitcher. Gently muddle jalapeño wheels with tequila using a wooden spoon. Add remaining three ingredients and stir gently. Garnish with extra jalapeño wheels and lime wedges. Pour into ice-filled glasses.

Mezcalada

MAKES 1 COCKTAIL

I love the smoky taste of mezcal with coconut and pineapple juice. For the less adventurous among us, feel free to substitute your favorite tequila for the mezcal.

1½ ounces mezcal
2 ounces coconut milk
2 ounces pineapple juice

½ ounce lime juice
Pineapple wedge or lime wheel, for garnish

Add ingredients to a shaker and fill with ice. Shake, shake, shake, and then strain into a tall glass filled with fresh ice. Garnish with pineapple wedge or lime wheel.

Hibiscus Mimosa

MAKES 6 MIMOSAS

Hibiscus, also known as Jamaica and Flor de Jamaica, is another favorite of mine. The flavor pairs well with bubbles, so pick your bottle of choice and get started!

Hibiscus syrup (page 103)
1 bottle chilled champagne, prosecco, or sparkling wine

Add desired amount of syrup to champagne flute, somewhere between ½ teaspoon to 1½ teaspoons seems to be about right, depending on your personal preference. Add bubbly of your choice, and serve!

Beet and Mango Licuado

SERVES 2

Licuados are a popular drink in Latin America that combine fruit, milk, and ice. My version omits the milk, instead using orange juice and beet to add color and flavor.

1 small beet, scrubbed and peeled, cut into small chunks
1 mango, peeled, pitted, and diced
½ cup orange juice, add more if a thinner consistency is desired
1 cup ice

Blend above ingredients together. Serve in tall glasses.

Pineapple Kale Juice

Pineapple Kale Juice

Pineapple Kale Juice is a favorite at my restaurants. It's an easy way to get your kale fix. To make a great mimosa, just add bubbly.

1 bunch kale, washed, ribs removed
2 cups canned pineapple chunks, with juice
5 cups orange juice

Purée kale and pineapple chunks in the bowl of a heavy-duty blender. Strain kale-pineapple mix with a fine wire mesh strainer. Get as much of the juice as possible. Discard the solids. Transfer juice to a pitcher, add orange juice, and serve over ice-filled glasses.

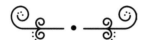

Guava Rum Punch for Two

SERVES 2

I love to serve this in a large bowl garnished with colorful fruit, lime wheels, and edible flowers.

½ cup gold rum
¾ cup guava purée, frozen and thawed, or guava nectar
¼ cup fresh lime juice
Edible flowers or fruit, for garnish

Mix first three ingredients in a pitcher or small bowl. Transfer to serving vessel and serve over ice.

Cafe de Olla

Cafe de Olla

I always order this delicious coffee when traveling in Mexico. In addition to cinnamon, other spices like cloves (just one, these are strong) or aniseeds work well together in this coffee.

4 cinnamon sticks
3/4 cup dark roast coffee, coarse grind
1/2 cup brown sugar or 6 ounces piloncillo
Orange peel, for garnish (optional)

Over medium heat in a saucepan, combine ingredients except for garnish with 5 cups of water. Bring to a slow boil. Stir occasionally to dissolve sugar. Remove from heat and let ingredients steep, about 5 minutes. Strain coffee through a fine-mesh sieve. Serve in cups or mugs and garnish with orange peel. Add a cinnamon stick to stir.

Mexican Hot Chocolate

MAKES 1 CUP

Mexican Hot Chocolate is a drink and dessert all wrapped into one. With canela (cinnamon) and just a hint of sweetness, this warm and comforting drink pairs well with Churros (page 137) in the morning or toasted bread. Or enjoy it on its own for the perfect end to an evening with family and friends.

2 tablespoons Mexican Chocolate (page 138)
6 ounces almond milk
Cinnamon, for garnish (optional)

Combine the Mexican Chocolate and the milk in a small saucepan. Heat the milk over a medium flame until steaming hot. Stir constantly so the milk is almost foamy. Serve in a mug and enjoy! Top with cinnamon, if desired.

Desserts

The reason I love Latin American food so much is because it is so bold and flavorful. This definitely goes for the desserts as well. I might go as far as saying a few of my favorite Latin American recipes *are* desserts!

If, like me, you love good chocolate, you'll find some great new recipes to explore. Don't forget to make the Cafe de Olla (page 123) for the perfect pairing anytime you serve something with chocolate!

Flourless Chocolate Cake with Salted Pepitas

SERVES 6

We have two Avas in the family—big A and little A, twelve and eight, respectively. They love to make this cake, and they do so on their own. The first couple of times, I walked them through it, but now they don't need me!

This cake can be made using two eight-inch springform pans or one twelve-inch springform pan. Either way, it's a good idea to have two large, flat metal spatulas handy to transfer the loosened cake to a platter or when adding the second layer. For novices, the one cake option is best. Unmolding this delicate cake and transferring it to a serving platter might seem scary, but, know this: even if your cake cracks or breaks, you can still put it together and when the chocolate ganache has frosted, no one will be able to tell the difference. Even if they could, they won't care, because this cake is that good!

If you don't like pepitas, feel free to omit them; this cake will still be amazing. It's good served warm, but it's also tasty when cold with a glass of bubbly!

2½ cups semisweet chocolate chips
2½ sticks (1½ cups) butter
¾ cup sugar
12 egg yolks
6 egg whites
Chocolate Ganache (page 138)
Salted Pepitas (recipe follows)

Preheat oven to 325°F.

Butter and sugar two 8-inch springform pans or one 12-inch springform pan. Melt the chocolate with the butter in a double boiler. When the butter starts to melt and the chocolate is beginning to look glossy, stir with a fork to combine. Set aside and let cool.

Divide the sugar between two mixing bowls. Add the egg yolks to one, and the egg whites to the other.

Using a stand mixer and clean beaters and bowl (if not thoroughly clean, the egg whites won't stiffen up), add the egg whites and sugar to the mixing bowl, and beat until soft peaks form. Transfer to another bowl.

Also with the stand mixer, beat the egg yolks and sugar until the mixture is pale and thick, about 4½ minutes.

Use a rubber spatula to scrape the beaten egg yolks into the melted chocolate, which should be cooled to room temperature by now. If not, wait, as you don't want to make scrambled eggs. Fold to combine. Then, gently fold the egg whites into the chocolate/egg yolk mixture. When well combined, pour into the prepared springform pan(s).

Bake for 25 to 35 minutes until the cake(s) top(s) looks dry and begin to crack. *Keep in mind that the two smaller cakes will take less time to cook than the one larger cake.*

While cake is cooking, prepare chocolate ganache and salted pepitas.

When cake has cooled, run the tip of a knife around the edge of the cake and open the springform pan. Remove the sides of the pan, and run a thin knife or thin metal spatula underneath the cake to loosen it from the pan. Transfer to serving platter. Pour desired amount of chocolate ganache on the top of the cake. If using one larger cake pan, you can sprinkle with pepitas. If doing two layers, after pouring ganache on top of the bottom layer, top with the second cake, pour and spread with remaining chocolate ganache, and then sprinkle with pepitas. This cake can be served warm, at room temperature, or cold.

Roasted Salt Pepitas

1 cup raw pepitas (pumpkin seeds)
2 teaspoons olive oil

1 teaspoon salt, more or less to taste (a coarse sea salt works nice)

Preheat oven to 375°F. In a small bowl, coat pumpkin seeds with oil. Transfer seeds to a cast-iron pan or rimmed baking sheet. Let pumpkin seeds roast in the oven until starting to brown about 10 minutes. Remove from oven, and carefully toss with salt.

Let cool and store in an airtight, preferably glass container.

Coconut Flan

SERVES 6

The creamy texture and irresistible tropical coconut flavor make even those who don't typically like flan love this one. Cream cheese makes for a firmer texture, tangier taste, and a somehow more delicious custard.

The smooth caramel top of a traditional coconut flan can be an intimidating feat to first-timers. While it does look and taste great, you can skip making it and just concentrate on the creamy sweet flan. But practice makes perfect when it comes to caramel, so give the syrup a whirl—but remember, hot syrup is extremely hot, so be careful, and don't let the kids help with that step.

1 cup sugar

1 (14-ounce) can coconut milk

1 (14-ounce) can sweetened
   condensed milk

1 (8-ounce) package cream cheese

Pinch of salt

6 large eggs, lightly beaten

Preheat oven to 325°F.

Place a 9-inch cake pan next to the stove. Place the sugar in a small, heavy saucepan and drizzle ⅓ cup of water evenly over. Place the pan over a medium flame and swirl the pot over the heat to mix and dilute the sugar and water. Continue swirling (don't stir) until completely dissolved (if it begins to brown before the sugar has completely dissolved, pull it from the heat). When a clear syrup has formed, cover the pot and cook for 2 minutes at a boil. Uncover, and swirl the pot again. The syrup should turn a dark amber color. Pour the bubbling syrup into the cake pan, tilting the dish to evenly spread the caramel.

In the bowl of an electric mixer, combine the coconut milk, condensed milk, cream cheese, and salt and beat until smooth. Add the eggs and mix on lowest speed until just combined. Pour into the cake pan.

Place the cake pan in a larger baking dish filled with enough water to reach halfway up the pan (about 1-inch). Place on the middle rack of the oven and bake for 60 minutes. Remove from oven, let cool to room temperature, and then chill for at least 4 hours.

To serve, place the flan in a large dish of hot water to loosen the caramel from the pan. Run a knife around the edges of the pan and then invert onto a serving plate. The caramel will run down the sides of the flan as you remove the cake pan. Serve immediately.

Pineapple Cobbler

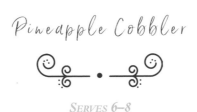

Less precise in its assembly than a pie, this cobbler is fun and fast to put together. The food processor makes foolproof dough every time. If pineapple isn't your thing, use whatever fruit or fruit combination you wish. Garnishing this cobbler with a few fresh berries is always nice!

2½ cups all-purpose flour + 2 tablespoons
¼ teaspoon salt
1 cup sugar + ½ cup
2 sticks unsalted butter, slightly softened
2 eggs
2 cups pineapple chunks, fresh, frozen, or canned

Preheat the oven to 350°F.

Pulse the 2½ cups of flour, salt, 1 cup of sugar, butter, and eggs in a food processor until they come together in a ball. Divide the dough into two equal-size pieces. (The dough can be made up to one day ahead, wrapped in plastic, and refrigerated until ready to use.)

Toss the pineapple with the remaining sugar and flour.

Using a 9-inch pie plate, use your fingers to press one piece of dough into a loose circle, covering the bottom of the plate. Spread ¾ of the fruit mixture over the dough. Press the remaining piece of dough into a circle (use a lightly floured cutting board) and layer the dough over the fruit. Top with the remaining fruit mixture.

Bake the cobbler in the oven until the crusts are golden brown and the fruit is bubbling, approximately 55 minutes.

Let the cobbler cool briefly before serving.

Mexican Chocolate Tamales

MAKES 24 TAMALES

Lucy has been making tamales for my restaurants for more than twenty years; her tamales are simply the best. She pays attention to detail and does everything with great care. Lucy has shared her secret to tamale making with me, and now I'll share it with you: the most important tip to making tamales that are light and airy is to have enough water in the dough. If the dough is too heavy, the tamales will be heavy. This recipe is for the more adventurous among you. Tamales take a bit of practice, but you'll get the hang of it. Once you do, chocolate tamales are the way to go. Traditionally, sweet tamales are filled with fruit, but I've made the switch to something everyone loves: chocolate.

1 (8-ounce) package dried corn husks
2 cups masa harina (see Sources, page 155)
2 sticks butter, softened a bit
¼ teaspoon baking powder
1 cup chocolate ganache + more to plate (page 138)
¼ cup cocoa powder
¾ cup Mexican Chocolate (page 138)
Fresh whipped cream, for serving (optional)

Select the biggest corn husks from the package and remove all strands of corn silk. Soak them in hot water until they are soft and pliable, about 30 minutes.

In the bowl of a stand mixer fitted with a paddle attachment, combine the masa, butter, ½ cup water, baking powder, 1 cup of the ganache (the remaining ganache will be used as a garnish), cocoa powder, and Mexican Chocolate. Mix until a *soft* dough forms (softer than Play-Doh). Add more water if necessary.

Drain the husk and pat dry. Lay a husk in your hand, narrow end toward you, smooth side up. Place 2 tablespoons of the chocolate masa in a log shape about 1 inch from the bottom and 2 inches from the top. Fold the two sides over the end of the tamale.

Stand the tamales in a steamer or a colander and cover with a lid. Steam the tamales over water for about 40 minutes, until the filling no longer sticks to the husk.

Serve the tamales while hot, each topped with a spoonful of ganache and a dollop of whipped cream, if desired.

Croissant Bread Pudding
with Mexican Chocolate and Almonds

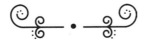

SERVES 6

Warm and delicious, bread pudding is always a crowd-pleasing dessert. This recipe elevates traditional bread pudding, using flaky croissants and tasty Mexican chocolate. Plan on serving this one warm from the oven.

With croissant sizes varying from bakery to bakery, you'll have to see how many fit into your pie pan.

2 tablespoons butter, softened

3 eggs

1½ cups half-and-half

2 tablespoons brown sugar

Croissants, enough to fill a 9-inch pie plate,
    split in half as for a sandwich

Mexican Chocolate (page 138)

1 cup sliced almonds

Preheat oven to 350°F.

Butter a 9-inch pie plate and set aside. Combine the eggs, half-and-half, and brown sugar in a large mixing bowl. Whisk to combine. Press the sliced croissants into the egg mixture and soak for 3 minutes, turning once or twice. They should absorb the egg mixture but not to the point of falling apart. Fit the bottom half of each croissant into the buttered pie plate, sliced-side down.

Sprinkle two-thirds of the Mexican Chocolate over the croissants and then half of the almonds. Layer the remaining halves of the croissants, sliced-side down again, over the bottoms. Sprinkle the remaining Mexican Chocolate and almonds over the top and transfer to the preheated oven.

Bake the bread pudding until puffy and dry on top but moist inside, 45 to 60 minutes.

Coconut Rice Pudding

Coconut Rice Pudding

For a good rice pudding, you have to start with the right type of rice. I find that a good-quality Chinese or Japanese short- or medium-grain rice works best. At first glance, it may seem like this recipe calls for a lot of liquid given the limited amount of rice, and it does. That's to achieve a creamy rice pudding. With patience you'll see the liquid reduce, and you'll achieve the perfect consistency.

¼ teaspoon salt

1 cup medium- or short-grain rice

4 cups whole milk

2 cans coconut milk (full fat)

1 cup sweetened condensed milk

Fresh berries, for garnish (optional)

Bring 3 cups of water to a boil in a medium saucepan. Add the salt and the rice, stir once, and reduce heat to a simmer. When the rice has absorbed most of the water, about 25 minutes, add the whole milk, coconut milk, and sweetened condensed milk. Stir to thoroughly combine.

Simmer the pudding over a medium flame, stirring occasionally until it begins to thicken, about 15 to 20 minutes. Begin stirring almost constantly and lower heat as the pudding continues to thicken to an oatmeal-like consistency. This can take up to 45 minutes over a medium-low flame. Remove from heat and let cool enough to spoon into individual serving bowls or glasses. Refrigerate until ready to serve, then garnish with berries if desired.

Tropical Fruit with Rum Honey Drizzle

A light, fun dessert for adults. Since the sauce has a hint of rum, don't be surprised if you run out of the sauce before you run out of fruit. If you do, it takes just a minute to whisk up more. If you've got a fun crowd for Sunday brunch, this is a must.

¼ cup honey

½ cup gold rum

1 cup raspberries

1 mango, diced

1 orange, cut into segments

1 kiwi, peeled and diced

1 red jalapeño chili, sliced thinly

¼ cup mint leaves, finely chopped

Combine the honey and rum and whisk until thoroughly blended. Set aside until ready to serve. Toss the fruit, jalapeño, and mint in a medium bowl and divide among six glasses or in desired serving container. Re-whisk Rum Honey Sauce just before serving and drizzle over fruit.

Bananas with Rum

SERVES 4

This is modern twist on the traditional Bananas Foster recipe. While it makes a fantastic and simple stand-alone dessert, you can also serve it alongside pancakes or French toast for a great addition to any brunch menu.

½ cup butter
¾ cup dark brown sugar
3 ripe bananas, peeled and cut into
　¼-inch slices

2 tablespoons orange juice, more as needed
½ cup dark rum
4 scoops vanilla ice cream
½ cup chopped peanuts (optional)

Combine the butter and brown sugar in a sauté pan over a medium heat. Swirl the pan until the mixture has started to thicken and caramelize, about 2 minutes. Adjust heat as needed so the caramel doesn't burn.

Add the bananas to the pan and stir to coat. Add the orange juice and when it is completely incorporated, about 20 seconds, turn off the heat. Add the rum and turn the heat back on. Simmer for about 2 minutes to cook away the raw alcohol taste.

Spoon the bananas over ice cream and then sprinkle each dish with some chopped peanuts, if desired. Serve immediately.

Chocolate Ganache and Fresh Fruit

SERVES 4–6

A simple but pretty dessert, this goes perfectly with a big main course. It is appreciated by all who want just a little something sweet after their meal.

Chocolate Ganache (page 138)
2 bananas, peeled and sliced
2 kiwis, peeled and sliced

1 pint raspberries
1 pint strawberries

Fill a small serving bowl with the Chocolate Ganache and place in the center of a large platter. Surround with the assorted fruits.

Churros with Raspberry Purée

SERVES 6

Churros are a delicious Latin treat that I lighten up with both fresh and puréed fruit. Wonderful for dessert, but it's also a great way to start the weekend—just add coffee and the morning paper.

½ cup (1 stick) unsalted butter

½ teaspoons salt

1 cup flour

3 eggs

Vegetable oil, for frying

1 cup sugar, more or less as desired

Raspberry Purée (page 111)

Heat the butter and salt with 1 cup of water in a medium-size saucepan. Bring to a boil over medium-high heat until butter has melted and mixture is at a hard simmer. Remove pan from the heat and add the flour all at once, stirring constantly with a heavy wooden spoon until combined and flour streaks are gone. Let the dough ball cool for 3 to 4 minutes. Transfer dough ball to the bowl of a stand mixer with the paddle attachment. Set to medium speed and add the eggs, one at a time, making sure each egg is fully combined before adding the next egg. Beat until the dough is combined, smooth, and shiny.

Fit a pastry bag with the star tip and fill with churro batter. Set aside for a minute while preparing the pan.

Heat 2 inches of oil in a large, straight-sided sauté pan over medium-high heat. Your pan is ready when small bubbles form at the bottom. If you're using a frying thermometer, the temperature should be 350°F.

Working in batches, carefully pipe churro batter into the hot oil, taking care not to crowd the pan. You can keep it simple and do lines of churros or get creative with a swirly design. The dough should sizzle but not spatter, so adjust heat as necessary. Fry the churros for about 2 minutes before turning. When they are golden brown on all sides, transfer them to a paper towel–lined tray to drain. Repeat with remaining dough.

Place the sugar in a brown paper bag and shake churros lightly to coat. Serve immediately with the Raspberry Purée.

CHURROS

Churros are log-shaped pieces of dough made with a piping bag that squirts the dough into hot oil. You can use a pastry bag with a medium-size open star tip or use a serving spoon to pull a trail of batter over the oil. I recommend using a thermometer for the oil.

Simple Chocolate Ganache

Use as a dip for fresh fruit, drizzle for pound cake, or sauce for ice cream.

2½ cups semisweet chocolate chips
¾ cup half-and-half

Heat the chocolate chips and half-and-half in the top of a double boiler over simmering water until chocolate is glossy and begins to melt. Stir with a fork until smooth.

If you don't have a double boiler, the microwave method works quite well: combine the chocolate chips and half-and-half in a microwavable bowl. Microwave on High at 30-second intervals, stirring in between until the chocolate has completely melted, about 1½ minutes.

The ganache can be used immediately or refrigerated until needed and reheated. Chocolate Ganache will last about a week in the refrigerator.

Mexican Chocolate

MAKES 1½ CUPS

Chocolate has always been an integral part of Latin food culture. Cocoa beans have been used in the past as currency, buried alongside leaders, and, of course, made into drinks, moles, and sweets. Both the Mayans and Aztecs flavored their chocolate, sometimes with honey, herbs, cinnamon, and chilies.

1 cup semisweet chocolate chips
½ cup sugar
1 tablespoon cinnamon

Combine the ingredients in a food processor and pulse. Store in a cool, dry place in an airtight container. If stored properly Mexican Chocolate will last a couple of months.

Cacao

I *love love love* chocolate. I don't gorge myself or anything like that, but I always have a few good-quality chocolate bars around and I break off little pieces throughout the day and eat them (almost every day). So when my good friend Monica asked me to go on a trip to check out cacao farms deep in the jungles in Tabasco, Mexico, I said *heck yea!* At the time, Monica and her husband, Tom, wanted to start a chocolate company, and Monica, who has always been very thorough, wanted to go and tour the cacao farms and learn as much as she could before they got to work. Currently, Monica and Tom make great tasting, single origin, bean-to-bar chocolate at Goodnow Farms Chocolate, which they run from behind their barn in Massachusetts. To create their single origin bars, they seek out farmers who grow cacao beans with the greatest flavor potential. Their search has taken them to remote villages and small family farms throughout Mexico, Central, and South America. They are firmly committed to ensuring that the cacao they source is ethically grown, that the farmers receive fair compensation, and that the farming methods used are sustainable. They work directly with their farmers and producers and have invested in some communities to improve product quality, and develop mutually beneficial relationships.

Breakfasts

I can't eat eggs without some kind of hot sauce or salsa. This combination makes Latin American food great for breakfast and even better for brunch. (Pass the Hibiscus Mimosa, please!) Don't forget about the sweet bite, too. Strawberry Mango Pancakes, anyone?

Strawberry Mango Pancakes

Who doesn't love pancakes? They are even easier to love when strawberries and mango are cooked into them.

2 cups all-purpose flour
¼ cup + 2 tablespoons sugar
½ teaspoon salt
3 teaspoons baking powder
2 cups milk
3 tablespoons butter, melted and then cooled slightly
2 eggs
1 mango, sliced
2 pints strawberries, sliced
Raspberry Purée (page 111)

Sift the flour, sugar, salt, and baking powder together. Combine the milk, butter, and eggs in a small bowl and whisk to combine. Add the wet ingredients to the dry and whisk until just incorporated.

Use a ladle to spoon batter onto the hot griddle. As one side cooks, drop mango and strawberry slices into each pancake. Flip the pancakes when air bubbles form, and then finish cooking the other side. Save some mango and strawberry slices to garnish the top and between the pancakes. Serve with maple syrup and a side of Raspberry Puree.

Breakfast Nachos

This is a fun, colorful, and easy brunch item. If you make your sauces and black beans the day before, the day-of prep will go much quicker. For bacon lovers, sprinkle a half pound of extra crispy chopped bacon over the cheese. Hibiscus Mimosas (page 118) go great with this.

6 eggs
1 large bag restaurant-style tortilla chips
2 cups shredded Jack cheese, more as desired oil to coat pan
Easy Crema (page 107)
Isabel Sauce (page 107)
Pickled Red Onion (page 69)
½ cup tomatoes, chopped
½ cup cilantro
Black Beans, (optional as a side (page 50))

Preheat oven to 350°F.

Crack eggs in a large bowl, whisk, and set aside while you put the chips in the oven. On a large, ovenproof platter, place a layer of tortilla chips, follow with a generous sprinkling of cheese, and repeat. Place in oven and bake for 10 minutes or until cheese is gooey and melted. While nachos are baking, coat a large pan with oil, heat to medium, and scramble eggs.

When nachos are finished cooking, remove from oven, and set on heatproof surface. To plate, place scrambled eggs over nachos, drizzle with Easy Crema and Isabel Sauce, and sprinkle red onion, tomato, and cilantro. Serve as soon as possible with black beans on the side, if desired.

Coconut and Raspberry Chia Breakfast Pudding

A heathy way to start the day! If you make it the day before, it's a great timesaver in the morning. Fresh fruit goes great and looks great with this layered when with chia pudding.

1 cup coconut milk (full fat, with all
    its creamy goodness)
½ cup chia seeds, divided
2 tablespoons maple syrup, divided
Raspberry Compote (page 111)
½ cup almond or hemp milk

Combine coconut milk, ¼ cup chia seeds, and 1 tablespoon maple syrup in a bowl. (Reserve the other ¼ cup of chia seeds and 1 tablespoon maple syrup for the raspberry chia pudding.) Stir until combined and set aside in the refrigerator.

For raspberry chia pudding, combine ½ cup raspberry compote, almond milk, remaining chia seeds, and maple syrup in a bowl and stir until combined.

Refrigerate both the coconut chia and raspberry chia at least 3 hours or best overnight. When a pudding like consistency has been achieved, layer each into mason jars as follows: a few spoonfuls of raspberry compote, followed by coconut chia pudding, followed by raspberry chia pudding, then a layer of fresh fruit, if desired.

Green Chili Eggs and Ham Breakfast Muffins

SERVES 6

These little eggy muffins are so cute—and tasty, too!

Olive oil
½ yellow onion, diced
2 Anaheim chilies, roasted, peeled,
   seeded, chopped

8 eggs
Salt
1 cup Jack cheese
½ cup Black Forest ham, chopped

Preheat the oven to 350°F.

Warm the olive oil in a medium sauté pan over medium heat. Add the onion and cook until tender and translucent. Stir in chopped anaheim chilies, remove from heat, and set aside. Whisk eggs with salt and then stir in Anaheim chili/onion mix, cheese, and ham. Lightly coat muffin cups with olive oil. Fill each of the muffin cups nearly to the top with the egg mixture.

Bake for 12 to 14 minutes, until the muffins are puffed up, firm, and starting to turn golden brown. Remove from the oven and let the muffins stand for a minute to set the eggs. Tap the muffins out of the cups. If they're a little stuck, run a knife around the edges.

Grilled Peaches
with Blackberries, Cilantro, and Mint

SERVES 4

Peaches are the perfect fruit to grill, but make sure they are ripe but firm. If they're mushy to begin with, they will only get mushier and difficult to remove from the grill.

Vegetable oil
4 ripe but firm peaches
1 pint fresh blackberries

Honey, to drizzle on fruit
2 tablespoons fresh mint, chopped
2 tablespoons fresh cilantro, chopped

Heat grill to medium high. Brush peaches with vegetable oil. When grill is hot, place peaches cut-side down until fruit has nice grill marks, about 3 to 4 minutes. Arrange on serving platter or individual serving vessels. Top with blackberries and a drizzle of honey and sprinkle with mint and cilantro.

Quinoa Breakfast Cereal

I love quinoa in the morning; it makes me feel good. If you make the quinoa ahead of time, this breakfast cereal is then super-fast to throw together in the morning.

1 cup quinoa, well rinsed and drained
¼ cup raisins
¼ teaspoon Himalayan salt
Hemp, almond, or soy milk butter
Maple syrup
Hemp, almond, or soy milk
1 tart green apple, chopped (optional)
½ cup walnuts, chopped (optional)

Place quinoa in a medium saucepan and cover with 2 cups cold water. Add raisins to the pot so they plump up while the quinoa is cooking. Sprinkle with Himalayan salt and bring to a slow boil over medium-high heat, then reduce heat to low so that the mixture simmers. Cook and cover until the water has been absorbed and the quinoa is tender, 15 to 20 minutes. When the quinoa is cooked, you will see tiny spirals in the grain.

Divide quinoa among bowls and top each bowl with a blob of butter, a drizzling of maple syrup, and a glug of hemp, almond, or soy milk. Finish it off with green apples and walnuts.

Plantain Hash Browns with Eggs and Black Beans

I like to make individual plantain hash browns in a small skillet (preferably cast iron). This will take a bit more time because you're making one at a time. If you want to be a real pro, use two small skillets simultaneously to finish the hash browns faster. If either of these two methods seems too daunting, feel free to use one big skillet and just cut the hash browns into pieces. If you do it this way, don't try to flip the whole thing at once when you're cooking; separate it into pieces and flip those.

3 green plantains
Vegetable oil, for frying
Sea salt
2 tablespoons butter or olive oil
8 eggs
Quick Black Beans (page 50)

Blot the plantains dry after peeling (for instructions on peeling plantains, see page 18). Cut plantains in long, thin strips as follows: cut each plantain into two pieces width-wise, then cut each of those pieces into three lengthwise pieces. Next, I lay each of those pieces flat and cut them into long strips. I try to get these thin but not so thin that they break apart or start to crumble.

Heat oil (oil should be about ¼ inch high in the pan) in a small sauté pan over a medium flame. When small bubbles form on the bottom of the pan, gently place plantains into the hot oil, following the shape of the pan. The oil should sizzle but not spatter, so lower or raise the flame accordingly. Cook until bottom side has crusted together and is a deep golden-brown color—you can use a metal spatula to check. Gently flip over when the bottom side is nice and crispy. Cook remaining side of the plantain. It's cooked through when it's deep golden and crispy throughout.

Transfer to a paper towel–lined tray to drain. Sprinkle with sea salt. Repeat until you have 4 crispy plantain hash browns. Set aside while frying eggs.

In a large skillet, heat the butter or olive oil until hot. Cook eggs as desired.

Transfer the cooked eggs to plates and serve alongside the plantain hash browns and black beans. Consider serving this dish with your favorite salsa or sauce. I am partial to Isabel Sauce (page 107).

Dragon Potatoes

This is a much in-demand breakfast side dish. Here, potatoes, like tostones, are twice cooked and smashed flat. Serve with eggs and a little Basic Salsa (page 93).

2 pounds red potatoes, unpeeled
Olive oil
2 red jalapeños, sliced into rounds
Salt
Black Beans (page 50)
1 cup grated Jack cheese
¼ cup green onion, thinly sliced on a diagonal
1 cup tomato, diced

Place the potatoes in a large pot of salted water and bring to a boil over a high flame. Cook until they are tender but still hold their shape, about 20 minutes. Drain, and set aside. When they are cool enough to handle, smash them with your hands so they are flattened and chunky.

Heat a small pan with 2 teaspoons of olive oil. Lightly sauté the jalapeños for about 1 minute, and then set aside until ready to serve.

Heat a large sauté pan over a medium flame. Add ¼ cup of olive oil (about 1 inch), and add the flattened potatoes. Cook potatoes until golden brown, about 6 minutes. Turn and continue cooking until the other side browns, about 6 more minutes. Replenish olive oil if necessary. Don't turn the potatoes until they have a nice golden crust. Salt potatoes to taste.

Transfer the potatoes to four serving plates. Top each with a scoop of black beans, a sprinkle of cheese, some green onion, and tomato. Garnish each with the sautéed jalapeños.

Thank You

A restaurant life is a crazy life; it can consume every part of you. I don't know if there are words enough to thank the amazing teams that run my restaurants. Without their hard work, I wouldn't have been able to write this book. Lucy, Amalia, Omar, and Carmelo—you have been with me since the beginning. Your attention to detail is what has made the food so good and so consistent for so many years. Jen M.—thank god for you, I would be a disorganized mess if it weren't for you. Thank you, Brian and Heather, for caring and doing such a great job. Thank you to my past managers who laid the groundwork—Gary John, Blaine, Sara O., Sara T, Pat South, Mark, Matt D, Callie and the Sieve brothers, Matt, and Patrick. I miss you all.

I don't think there is another city that has such a supportive culinary community. I have had such a great time with all of you! You work so hard and give so much, but you still have time for a good time. A special thanks to Flor Franco and Michelle Lerach— you two have taken it upon yourselves to unite this San Diego pirate ship of chefs, restaurateurs, farmers, butchers, fishermen, distributors, etc. You have created events, given everything you have for charity causes, and have thrown some of the best parties this town has ever seen. Thank you for getting us all together. and for your great work with the Berry Good Foundation.

Thank you to my amazing group of friends. Some of you I have known for more than thirty years—Christy, Carla P, Carla G, Shawn, Jamie, John, Monica, Pepper, Lulu, Dan, Maria H, Sam and Carolyn Kates. Thank you, Kalisa, for making such good food; I love being invited to your house to eat! Thank you, Naomi and Rolando, you are the most generous and gracious Latin hosts I know.

Thank you, Jaime Fritsch, for your great eye; you are a talented photographer. Thank you, Neens; you have been there throughout the years. You are creative and talented and have always come through for me. Thank you to my new friends, Alisa (you are a great foodie) and McCauley and Bernadette—you both have done such a great job.

My familia: Mom, Tita, Lee, Julie, Coby, Ava, Erik, Dena, Jackson, Ava, Vaughn, and Edgar. Thank you all for all the meals cooked and shared together and for how much you all love to eat!!! To the three men in my life: Robbie and Ryan, you have come such a long way. Thank you for turning out so good and helping me through thick and thin. Chris, you are such a good man; you work so hard and you still are always there for me! Love you all!!!!!

Sources

I tried to use ingredients in this book that are easy to find. Most grocery stores have a Latin section with simple varieties of fresh and dried chilies, chili powders, and basic spices. For the few things that are a bit harder to find we are lucky to live in a time where just about everything is available online. As most everyone knows, Amazon has a wealth of world products available in just days. Below I listed some great Latin food websites. One of my favorites is The Spanish Table, I am a sucker for clay cookware, which they have in addition to Spanish food products. I have used The Spice House for Szechuan peppercorns, which I think might be the hardest-to-find ingredient that I use in this book. Perfect Puree is another of my favorite sites; if you want to make a special cocktail for a party they have amazing purees to choose from. Plantains might be difficult to find in some places; for that I would look online for a list of Mexican markets or Latin markets in your area. Always call ahead to make sure they have what you are looking for.

SALSA EXPRESS
(800)-437-2572
www.salsaexpress.com
Salsas, chilies, and other fiery foods

THE SPANISH TABLE
(510)-548-1383
www.spanishtable.com
Great Spanish, Portuguese, and world ingredients

CUBAN FOOD MARKET
(877)-999-9945
www.cubanfoodmarket.com
As the name suggests: everything Cuban

AMIGO FOODS

(800)-627-2544

www.amigofoods.com

Largest online grocery store for food products all over Latin America

THE PERFECT PUREE

(707)-261-5100

www.perfectpuree.com

Excellent selection of purees to use for sauces etc. . . . Especially good for cocktails, their Pink Guava Puree is delish.

THE SPICE HOUSE

(312)-676-2414

www.thespicehouse.com

Wonderful selection of spices, including Szechuan peppercorns

ANDRES LATIN MARKET

1249 Morena Blvd, San Diego, CA 92110

(619)-275-6523

Great selection of spices and packaged foods from Latin American countries

Index

Conversion Charts

METRIC AND IMPERIAL CONVERSIONS
(These conversions are rounded for convenience)

Ingredient	Cups/Tablespoons/Teaspoons	Ounces	Grams/Milliliters
Butter	1 cup = 16 tablespoons = 2 sticks	8 ounces	230 grams
Cheese, shredded	1 cup	4 ounces	110 grams
Cream cheese	1 tablespoon	0.5 ounce	14.5 grams
Cornstarch	1 tablespoon	0.3 ounce	8 grams
Flour, all-purpose	1 cup/1 tablespoon	4.5 ounces/0.3 ounce	125 grams/8 grams
Flour, whole wheat	1 cup	4 ounces	120 grams
Fruit, dried	1 cup	4 ounces	120 grams
Fruits or veggies, chopped	1 cup	5 to 7 ounces	145 to 200 grams
Fruits or veggies, pureed	1 cup	8.5 ounces	245 grams
Honey, maple syrup, or corn syrup	1 tablespoon	0.75 ounce	20 grams
Liquids: cream, milk, water, or juice	1 cup	8 fluid ounces	240 milliliters
Oats	1 cup	5.5 ounces	150 grams
Salt	1 teaspoon	0.2 ounce	6 grams
Spices: cinnamon, cloves, ginger, or nutmeg (ground)	1 teaspoon	0.2 ounce	5 milliliters
Sugar, brown, firmly packed	1 cup	7 ounces	200 grams
Sugar, white	1 cup/1 tablespoon	7 ounces/0.5 ounce	200 grams/12.5 grams
Vanilla extract	1 teaspoon	0.2 ounce	4 grams

OVEN TEMPERATURES

Fahrenheit	Celsius	Gas Mark
225°	110°	¼
250°	120°	½
275°	140°	1
300°	150°	2
325°	160°	3
350°	180°	4
375°	190°	5
400°	200°	6
425°	220°	7
450°	230°	8